The Gospel and Authority
a P.T. Forsyth Reader

The
Gospel
and
Authority

a P.T. Forsyth Reader

**Edited by
Marvin W. Anderson**

AUGSBURG PUBLISHING HOUSE · MINNEAPOLIS, MINNESOTA

THE GOSPEL AND AUTHORITY:
A P. T. FORSYTH READER

Contents

Foreword

Peter Taylor Forsyth is now widely recognized as an important
and prophetic figure among the relatively few notable Noncon-
formist divines in the first decades of the twentieth century.
Amid the strong tides of liberal theology, his sermons and his
discourses struck out in another direction. His positive Christo-
logical affirmations and his view of the atonement seemed to
anticipate some of the affirmations, in a different context, which
were to come from Karl Barth. And though our present stress
is to run from Barth to a radicalism which represents much of
an older liberalism, Forsyth's emphases are still timely and modern. It seems likely that he will take his place, with figures like
Robertson of Brighton—among preachers and theologians who
will be read profitably for many generations to come, not on
grounds of theological antiquarianism, but as speaking that language of the centuries which makes all Christians contemporary.
For that reason we must warmly welcome an anthology of his
writings, and be grateful to its learned editor.

GORDON RUPP
Dixie Professor of
Ecclesiastical History in the University of
Cambridge

Preface

Not until graduate study in Aberdeen, Scotland, did the name Peter Taylor Forsyth arrest my attention. There, in Forsyth's birthplace, Professor A. M. Hunter lent me his unpublished notes on Forsyth and his biblical insights. Those notes, later published in *Teaching and Preaching the New Testament* (1964), showed Forsyth's genius. As one Aberdeen minister remarked, "There is more of the gospel in Forsyth than in all of continental theology."

Recently there has been a resurgence of interest in Forsyth, and a number of excellent studies have been undertaken. The essay by Professor Hunter and a chapter in J. K. Mozely's *The Heart of the Gospel* are superior. Winthrop Stewart's doctoral thesis, written at Aberdeen in 1965, is also excellent though unpublished, and I am indebted to it.

These studies point to the continuing significance of Forsyth's theology. Dissent's greatest theologian will continue to gain a hearing wherever (like St. Paul in Galatians 6:14) men are radical enough to seek after the cross.

While teaching two courses in Forsyth's theology at Bethel Seminary in St. Paul, Minn., I came to agree with a suggestion of Professor Hunter that the best of Forsyth was yet to be reprinted. Working under a grant from the Alumni

9

Council of Bethel College and Seminary in 1967, I consulted with Dr. Hunter, who guided the selection with an eye to contemporary theological issues. Principal John Marsh, D.D., of Mansfield College, Oxford, graciously shared his personal library and knowledge of Forsyth. Rev. John Huxtable, chairman of the Independent Press and minister secretary of the Congregational Church in England and Wales, evaluated the selections. As author of *Revelation Old and New*, his experience, judgment and encouragement are evident throughout the book.

I would also like to thank Rev. Gordon S. Wakefield, editor of the *London and Holburn Quarterly Review;* Mr. A. M. Jakeway of the Epworth Press; Miss Joy Hill and Mr. Rayner Unwin of George Allen and Unwin Ltd.; and Mr. Dominic LeFoe of the *Contemporary Review* for releasing publication rights to the essays. Professor Hunter supplied his own unpublished lectures on Forsyth's ethics and a similar lecture on the atonement by Professor David Cairns. Donn Michael Ferris, librarian of Duke University Divinity School, sent information on Ray Allen's unpublished Ph.D. thesis of 1953, "The Christology of P. T. Forsyth."

Items reprinted from the *Contemporary Review* are copyrighted by the editor. Items reprinted from the *Hibbert Journal* are copyrighted by George Allen and Unwin Ltd. Items reprinted from the *London Quarterly Review* are copyrighted by the Epworth Press. Spellings and capitalizations have been changed to conform to American style, otherwise the essays are reprinted according to the originals.

MARVIN W. ANDERSON

Introduction

In May, 1848, Peter Taylor Forsyth was born, the eldest child of a hard working couple in Aberdeen. Though thrifty, intelligent, and deeply concerned about spiritual matters, they never were able to rise above poverty. His mother was of highland heritage, and his father lowland, a deacon of Blackfriars Street Congregational Church.

Forsyth was never a strong child, but this did not prevent him from taking part in snowball fights and school games. At age fourteen he won the decisive struggle on the road to education. A bursary from the six hundred year old grammar school led him to the university. In 1864 he was dux of the grammar school which had numbered Lord Byron amongst its former pupils. After five years of brilliant prize taking, Peter Taylor Forsyth graduated M.A. with first class honors in the classics.

In 1870 Forsyth and a friend reopened a Congregational chapel which had been emptied by preaching. They drew large congregations. After a year of assisting the teaching of classics in the university, at the urging of Robertson Smith, he went to Göttingen for a semester of study under Albrecht Ritschl. This study in 1870 was the most significant intellectual development in his life. "Not only was his

mind developed by the philosopher, but he succeeded in
acquiring a facility and fluency in German thought and
language which he kept up all his life; it was one of his
few naive vanities that when traveling in later years he
was always mistaken for a German." [1]

Forsyth on return from Germany studied at New College,
London, for the Congregational ministry. Ill health forced
him to miss regular attendance at lectures, and he was
allowed to withdraw at his own request. Forsyth then accepted the call of the Congregational church at Shipley, a
suburb of Bradford in Yorkshire, where for ten years from
1874 to 1884 he began the first of five pastorates. From
Shipley he went to St. Thomas's Square in Hackney, London, where he plunged into the social milieu and gave
crowded Sunday evening lectures on art, politics, and the
theatre. It was at Cheetam Hill in north Manchester from
1885-1888 that a more serious note crept into Forsyth's
preaching. There his first book was published, *Pulpit Parables for Young Hearers*.[2] The style, though a bit self-con-
scious in this first book, altered dramatically as Forsyth experienced a conversion, or "miraculous entry upon the
Christian life." [3] From Manchester he went to Leicester
(1888-1893), and to Emmanuel Church, Cambridge, in
1894. Three weeks after arriving in Cambridge his wife
died, and for three years he lived in sorrow and depression
alone with his daughter, too ill to journey to Aberdeen in
1895 to receive the honorary D.D. conferred upon him by
the university.

While at Cambridge Forsyth began a remarkable career

---

[1] Jessie Forsyth Andrews, "Memoir" in *The Work of Christ* (London:
Collins Fontana Library, 1965), p. 14.

[2] See the selections in Harry Escott, *Peter Taylor Forsyth (1848-1921)
Director of Souls* (London: The Epworth Press, 1948), pp. 107-118. Prin-
cipal John Marsh of Mansfield College, Oxford loaned me his copy of
Pulpit Parables. I concur in Escott's judgment.

[3] See Robert M. Brown, "The Conversion of P. T. Forsyth," *Congregational Quarterly* XXX (1952), 237.

of theological creativity which in 1896 served to dramatize that turning point in his thought. Ten years later at Yale he commented on the change noted by the hearers of his sermon at Leicester in 1896, "God the Holy Father." The solid preparation for that sermon is the book *Charter of the Church,* also published in 1896.

A second marriage while at Cambridge rescued Forsyth from despair and sent him in healthier spirits to the principalship of Hackney College, Hampstead, London in 1901. The 1899 sermon at Tremont Temple to the second decennial International Congregational Council on the theme, "The Evangelical Principle of Authority," marks this healthy theological period. Forty years later J. D. Jones could remember that address with these remarks:

> It was in the address of Dr. Forsyth that the council reached its climax. . . . His paper resolved itself into a passionate plea for the Cross as the central thing in our Christian faith. I heard Forsyth on many an occasion both before and after. But I never felt thrilled by him as I did that day. He spoke as a man inspired. He flamed, he burned. He came after two rather dry and arid addresses. He brought us back to the heart of things.[4]

In London Forsyth threw himself into academic work and gave himself to his students. His literary style in this period leads many to discount his work. His daughter put it well when she said, "the real stumbling block is the idiom of his mind, rather than of his pen." [5] Recent writers appreciate Forsyth's constructive work apart from difficulties they may have with his style.

In an interview of January, 1907, by a reporter from the *Daily Mail,* R. J. Campbell, minister of City Temple in London sparked a bitter controversy over the new theology. In

---

[4]Quoted by Professor David Cairns of Aberdeen in an unpublished lecture on Forsyth which much of this sketch follows in outline.

[5]"Memoir," p. 27.

a book of 1907 titled *The New Theology*, Campbell argued for the natural religiousness of man with its source in God's ubiquitous presence. Forsyth responded in the pages of the *British Weekly* for March 7, 1907. Langford says that the most important rejoinders were made by the two most substantial theologians of the age, P. T. Forsyth and Charles Gore.

The war depressed Forsyth because of his deep love for Germany and its people, though he had no time for the pacifism of his students. In the four year period he published six books and a great many articles. Never really well any day of his life, Peter Taylor Forsyth died on November 11, 1921.

A fresh voice in British theology sounded with Forsyth in Cambridge in 1896. Could a reading of Forsyth fifty years after his death turn modern theology from its borderlands to the heartland of the cross? It is well worth the effort to inquire into the writings of one who could say in 1909:

> If life be a comedy to those that think, and a tragedy to those that feel, it is a victory to those that believe.

1. The Evangelical Churches and the Higher Criticism

Horton Davies calls Forsyth, "Dissent's greatest twentieth century theologian."[1] It is fitting that the Holy Communion service of Clare College, Cambridge, quotes from P. T. Forsyth. There in the center of creative and dissenting theology Forsyth served from 1894 until 1901 as minister of Emmanuel Church. While at Cambridge he wrote an essay on communion in which he said:

> In private worship we are apt to be self-engrossed. In public we are too dependent on the leader of the devotion, or the preacher who strives to kindle the common flame. In the communion (especially if it is to be in any extent liturgical), the leader sinks away, becomes but the voice, becomes the echo of a voice, whose echoes have been multiplied in every age, the channel of the voice of Jesus walking in calm light upon the world's wild waves, "Come unto me."

Will contemporary biblical criticism permit one so to worship? Forsyth turned to this most crucial problem for his times in 1905.

In this essay Forsyth faces squarely the implications of the collapse of belief in an inerrant Bible for the churches. It has been a good thing, claims Forsyth, for it has enabled people to see the spiritual authority of the gospel. Christ is

---

[1]Horton Davies, *Worship and Theology in England from Newman to Martineau*, 1850-1900 (London: Oxford University Press, 1962), p. 239.

15

the purpose of historic grace, the "ground of religion" as
Forsyth later put it in *The Principle of Authority*.

> The precious thing is not the historic fact of Christ,
> but the historic Word of him, the apostolic Word con-
> cerning Christ, the interpretation of the manifestation,
> the supramundane burden and interior of the fact.[2]

The highest criticism is a synthetic criticism by theologians,
not scholars. So it is a company of preachers, not a jury of
historians to whom we owe the tradition of Jesus. The pattern is Christ's own use of his Bible, the Old Testament. He
used his Bible "as a means of grace, not as a manual of
Hebrew or other history." Christ found there "not the
making of history by men, but the saving of history by
God."

No more crucial issue faces some contemporary theologians if one reads *Christianity Today* or the *Bulletin of the
Evangelical Theological Society*, both published in the
United States. In section XIV of this article Forsyth wrote
about the need for an authentic biblical theology:

> What we need from the scholar equipped with the
> soundest results, however new, is what Jonathan Ed-
> wards gave his day, a history of redemption, a history
> of the revelation always welling up through the religion
> of Israel and of Christendom at once purifying it and
> condemning it.[3]

❋   ❋   ❋

From the *Contemporary Review*
88 (1905)

I.

The great question of the age in all moral matters is the
question of a spiritual authority. It is not one which occupies

---

[2]p. 144.
[3]*Contemporary Review* 88 (1905), p. 598 and below.

the order for the day, but it does constitute the problem of time. The democracy is but little conscious how much it needs it, and it is not easy to secure its discussion in the forum of the churches. But it is their standing or falling article all the same. Some of them resent the idea of authority in any real and effective sense; some overdrive it; while others consider they possess it in the canon of Scripture. Now it is as true that the canon is not the authority as it is that without an authority beyond itself no church can go on existing.

Why may we not say that the final authority for church and creed is the Bible? Because there remains the question, *Is there anything that is over the Bible?* And to that question may I at once reply in advance that there is, and that:

1. It is not something which comes up to the Bible from without, like the scientific methods of historic research. To make that supreme and final would be pure rationalism. As the higher criticism it has its place, but it is a subordinate place.
2. It is something which is in the Bible itself, provided by it, and provided nowhere else. We must go back to the Bible to find what the Bible goes back to.

In a word, *that is over the Bible which is over the church. It is the gospel.* The gospel of God's historic act of grace is the infallible power and authority over both church and Bible. It produced them both. They both exist for its sake, and must be construed in its service. For both it is the great canon of interpretation as well as of organization, of Scripture, creed, and praxis. It was not the church that produced the Bible, nor the Bible that produced the church, but it was the gospel that produced both. It is of the greatest practical moment to realize this at present. It is our free church answer to a plausible claim that is urged by the Episcopal church to be the sole authoritative teacher of the Bible, because the church produced it at the first, and has therefore a hereditary monopoly of the *charisma veritatis*. We deny the fact behind the inference. Even were the Anglican church the church that selected the canon, no church produced the Bible. Both the Bible and the church are products of the gospel, which we preach as purely as they do, and mostly more so. Hence no church has the control of the Bible, but only a stewardship of it. The Bible needs no warrant from the church, only a witness. The gospel needs no application by the sacraments, only a fresh appropriation where it has been long applied by the Holy Ghost. Of course the Bible, on its part, must not arrest the church, but perpetually emancipate and inspire it. Luther by the Bible delivered us from the bondage of the church. But there are ways of treating the Bible which make us welcome the man or the movement that by the gospel will deliver us from the Bible.

But why not say that the something which is in and over the Bible is Christ? Because it is not quite certain what is covered by that word Christ. What do you mean by Christ? Is it Christ the character, chiefest among ten thousand and altogether lovely, or Christ the atoning Redeemer? *What is it that is authoritative in Christ?* Not his mere manner, as it subdued those who would arrest him. Not his far more than Socratic dignity of soul and insight. There is something in Christ which is over him. Well, you recognize that. It was his Father. You say readily, Christ was there not for his own sake, but his Father's. Yes, but that is far from enough. What was the relation between Christ and his Father? Was it a relation of the heart alone, of affection and rapt communion, as between the simple Madonna and the child? That is a common idea, and it enfeebles much faith. It makes Christ's piety the work of God, but does it assure us that his gospel was? The deeply devout or the wholly devoted may be lacking in the moral insight required for a real gospel. Was Christ's death due to the fact that he was

so purely and raptly pious? Was the cross simply the revenge
of the coarse Israel on the fine? Surely it took more than that
to make the death of Christ Israel's crime? His piety alone
would rather have made the Jews honor him as a finer
rabbi. Surely his dealing with his Father was more than
devout enjoyment, more than mystic union, more than the
practice of the presence of God and the culture of his own
soul? The personal unity had a practical, intelligible theme,
an exchange of thought, work, and purpose in relation to
the historic situation. It was not his Father's *love* he realized
only, it was his purpose of historic *grace,* his age-long purpose with the nation, his world-wide purpose with our race
—just as it was not the simple love of his brethren that lay
on him, but their burden, their curse. His Father gave him
not only a faith to cherish, a love to enjoy, but a vast and
old design to fulfill. Christ speaks far oftener of the will and
kingdom of God than of the heart of God. He was one with
a God who had been working for historic Hebrew centuries
to a certain holy and public purpose. And what was over
Christ was not simply the Father but the Father's holy
work with Israel for the world. What ruled his word and
deed was God's old historic purpose and long prophetic
gospel. The authoritative thing in him was God's *grace,*
God's holy grace. When we go to the Bible we find it is
to this the Bible goes. From this its breath comes; and its
soul incessantly returns to the gospel of grace that gave it.
And this is the test, the standard, the authority over the
Bible.

Of course you may say that Christ *is* God's gospel, and
purpose, and grace. And that is quite right, so long as we
are not speaking of the Jesus of biography, of Jesus as a
personal influence merely, but of the Christ of great history,
the Messiah of redemption; so long as we are not speaking
of the teaching and character of Christ only but of his work,
which was the crisis of his person; so long as we live and

move in Christ the Redeemer; so long as we do not begin
with the incarnation but end there; so long as we begin
with the redemption, atonement, reconciliation, and go on
to end in such an incarnation as is demanded for the purposes of that gracious gospel and that saving God; so long
as we recognize that "his work was his person in action" and
his person "his work in power." God was in Christ evangeli-
cally rather than metaphysically. He was in Christ reconciling. Faith believes in an incarnation required by the gospel,
however thought may set forth an incarnation required by
the nature of a divine idea. To begin with such an incarnation instead of with redemption is one of the most cardinal
and prolific errors of our time, as Bishop Creighton shrewdly
said.

II.

The testimony of Jesus is the spirit of prophecy. The purpose of Jesus is the purpose of history; or rather it is God's
purpose with history. The gospel of grace in Christ, the
purpose, and at last the act, of redemption is the key to the
Bible. It makes the Bible not a mere chronicle, not a mere
set of annals, but history of the greatest kind.

By history of the greatest kind I mean this. I mean something above even what we call the greater, the philosophic
history. May I explain? *What is it that raises the historian
above the annalist?* Is it not that the historian makes the
dumb facts speak which the annalist compiles? He sets the
facts in a whole, in a science, in a process, a principle, which
he makes them serve. He explains the facts. He turns them
into "signs." How? By some principle dawning out of them
upon his insight. By some deep, wide, and happy induction.
His spirit moves on the face of their chaos and elicits a
world. In other words, *he "places" the facts by means of a
hypothesis* they suggest, a theory. Of course, if he bring
his hypothesis from some other set of facts, or some other

kind, and force it on the facts under his eye, he is no true historian. But he is if he elicit it from the facts he handles. But you say, a true scientific historian is surely more than a hypothesis-monger. But really he is not. Are you not depreciating the place of hypothesis in life? It has not the value, of course, of absolute knowledge, but it has the value of explaining facts, of making them serve thought. And it is corroborated by all the subsequent facts. It is therefore, surer than the facts alone; and it paves the way for more certainty. What is science but a triumphal procession of hypotheses? In every science you have such a hypothesis or axiom as the base of fresh knowledge. The great law of nature's uniformity is a vast hypothesis which has on its side the whole of our knowledge and practice. But it is not an absolute truth. So with evolution, and with all the theories which set the world forth as an order or a process. And we conduct our life and business under such well-founded hypotheses as these, though it is *possible* they might not be true tomorrow. The sun might not rise. One day it will not. Now what the physicist does for nature the historian does for society. He interprets it by hypotheses which rank often among our great certainties as to the world's course.

But no hypothesis, no law of nature or history can give us the mind of God. God alone can do that. And when he does it is not discovery of ours, but revelation of his. It is not induction, not intuition even, but manifestation, the Word of the Lord. Christ's sense of God was not a vast surmise, sublime, but provisional and superable. It was not a great divination of his, behind which we may go and ask if he divined correctly. It was not man reaching God. The movement was quite otherwise. It was God reaching man. In Christ we have the culmination of the long revealing line of Old Testament prophecy. We have in a whole permanent personality what the prophets had but in their fleeting vision and burden. We have God seeking, and finding, and saving us. God tells us, through man's word, or by his own deeds, the secret of his purpose, his deep decrees and universal will. It is a purpose, will, and work of grace, of love, of redemption, of salvation. To carry home this is the object of the Bible. For this the Bible exists. From this the Bible sprang. *The place that is taken in human histories by hypothesis, theory, or law of progress is taken in the Bible by God's action, by revelation, by the gospel.* In the Bible we have the movement of the great lines and designs by which God treats the race and guides its total career. And especially we have the purpose and method of a Messiah, culminating in the redemption by Christ. It is his redemption that makes Jesus the Christ, and precious. The fact of Christ's life would be valueless (except to the historian of religion); the fact of his death would be of little moment (except to the martyrologist), apart from its function between man and God, its revealed meaning, its theological meaning, as atonement, redemption, reconciliation. These values are not got at by an induction. They are not won by flesh and blood, but revealed from the Father in heaven, as Christ himself told Peter. They are God's word to man, not man's hypothesis about God. That is a unique thing about the Bible among books. The gospel it contains is not a result of man's divining power over intractable facts, but it is the act and power of God unto salvation. The invisible realities are not guessed, they are actually conveyed through the things that appear. The gospel message is not a product of biblical theologians inducting from a study of religious phenomena which they found and formulated from these records. But it seizes us out of the Bible, it descends on us from the Bible as a power. It descended on the men who wrote the Bible. It was with the church that selected the Bible. It made the Bible in that way, and in that way it makes us from out the Bible. The soul of the Bible is not a crystallization of man's divinest idea; it is not even a divine declaration of what God is in himself; it is his revelation of what he is *for us* in actual history, what he for us has done, and forever does. It contains God's gift, not of knowledge, but of his gracious self. Revelation is futile as a mere exhibition. It is ineffectual except as redemption. God's Word is authoritative because it is more, it is creative. It is life from the dead. Its authority does not simply stand over us either as an imperative or as an ideal. It comes as a gospel. It comes with power to bring itself to pass in our new life. The God who rules us in Christ is not a foreign power. Theonomy is not heteronomy. He, our law, becomes also our life. He comes with something more even than authority over us, he comes with power in us. His authority is not simply impressive, it is enabling. *Dat quod jubet.* It is the power *of the Spirit,* not revealing alone, but redeeming us to take in the revelation. His Spirit does not seize us but lives in us. The Savior Son is revealed in us. Christ is our life who is also our Lord. His authority is not simply an external power, but a life-giving spirit within. We are redeemed into the power to know, to be, and to do what is revealed. And both the revelation and the redemption are one and the same act.

III.

To apply the gospel as the standard of the Bible is something higher than the higher criticism. It is the highest. It was by this test of the gospel that Luther dealt so boldly with the Epistle of James. It was not by literary criticism, where, like his age, he was not bold. And this is the only principle which gives the higher criticism, the literary and historic criticism, its true place. The church will never give that criticism its rights till she feels she is not at its mercy, till she is set free to do so by her gospel. You cannot secure freedom from a state or a church in a panic. And panic is the state of mind produced by scientific criticism, especially

on people who have long been putting the Bible narrative
in the place which belongs only to the Bible gospel. The
critical treatment of the Bible must have its place. Let us
not make fools of ourselves by denying it. We shall be
fighting against God and resisting the spirit. It arises out
of the sound principle of interpreting the Bible by itself.
Scriptura sui ipsius judex et interpres was the Reformer's
maxim. But its place is secondary, ancillary. It has little
place in a pulpit. Criticism is the handmaid of the gospel
—downstairs. The critical study of Scripture is at its best,
and the higher criticism is at its highest, when it passes from
being analytic and becomes synthetic. And the synthetic
principle in the Bible is the gospel. The analysis of the
Bible must serve the history of grace. The synthetic critic
is not the scholar but the theologian. The book is a witness
not of man's historical religion, but of God's historical redemption. It is not so much a record as a testimony. "Search
the Scriptures. Ye do well. They testify of me," not, record
me, not, report me, not, evidence me, but testify of me,
preach me, present me as the gospel. *The Bible is at its
highest as the preacher.* And it does not preach itself, or
its inerrancy, but the grace of God. It contains in this gospel
its own supreme principle of criticism and interpretation.
The church is the true interpreter of the Bible if it let the
Bible interpret itself. And for this purpose it repudiates the
modern mind, no less than the tradition of the church, as
its final court. The Bible comes to its own in the gospel
which made it what it is. This gospel survives all our critical
readjustments of the process by which it came. Indeed, it
emerges the more clearly from many of these reconstruc-
tions. The critics have restored the prophets, for instance,
to the service of the gospel as well as to the interest of the
church. And they have inflicted eternal death on books like
Keith and Newton, which made prophecy historical conun-
drums. But the gospel is not at the mercy of scientific

criticism, because the Bible is not a mere document. It is
a sacrament. It is more than a message of grace, it is a
"means of grace." It is more than a source of information,
it is an agent of saving experience. It is the former only as it
becomes the latter. That is to say, it is to faith rather than
to research that its facts become certainties. What Christ
did for us becomes sure by what he does in us. And *it is
vain to try and establish the Bible's real value by historical
canons without realizing the experience of its grace.*

Our moral need cannot wait for our historical critics. *The
Bible is not merely a record of the revelation; it is part of
the revelation.* It is not a quarry for the historian, but a
fountain for the soul. Its first work is not a vouch for the
fact of Jesus. As a voucher of that kind its value is secondary. We have nothing written by Jesus, nothing with
absolute certainty written by an eye-witness of Jesus. In
strict history Paul is nearer and clearer than Christ; but
Christ is the greater certainty to us none the less. Nor is
the Bible's first work to reflect the first church. The New
Testament, the epistles of Paul, are not a set of ideas or
sentiments stirred in certain minds by the historic contem-
plation of Christ, the mere reflection of Christ mirrored in
the shining consciousness of those nearest him. It is not
adequate to say that in the New Testament we have the
impression made by Christ upon the first church. We have
that, but we have more. We have Christ continuing to
teach, and lead, and save. We have a finished redemption,
energizing as revelation. We have the heavenly Christ revealing himself to and through the first church of the
redeemed. Indeed, I would rather say through the first
apostles. For they were not the representatives of the
church; they did not owe their place to its consent; nor
were they its organs so much as Christ's organs to it. *That
theory of impression is not the true full nature of inspiration.*
The whole of the New Testament is a continuation of

prophecy. It is the last of the prophets. It is not a document, but an appeal. It is a mighty sermon on Christ, not
an image of him, not a disquisition on him. Doubtless
Christ is the center. He is the fact. But the New Testament did not come into evidence to guarantee that fact to
rigid inquiry. It is not an arsenal of Christian evidences.
In that case the testimony would have been more careful.
And then also the historic sense would take faith's place,
and the historical experts would be the true Christian priest-
hood. The New Testament, like the Old Testament, is
history with a purpose, a bias. It has in it not only reliable
historical matter, but also the principle for construing it.
It has the bias of the will to save and not only the will to
believe. And it has the bias not only of the will to believe,
but of the belief that wills, that urges itself, that acts from
the will upon the evidence in a selective way, and forces
it on mankind.

IV.

Christ came for something else than to be a statuesque
fact, or even a teacher of supreme religious genius and
personal influence. *It is not the fact but the meaning of the
fact that matters.* He came for a practical crucial *purpose,*
historic and divine. He is valuable, not like a work of art
for what he is, but for what he means as God's gift. Indeed,
he is precious not for what he means even, but for what
he did in God's name. Nay, when we see this, when we
realize that we have in Christ the manifestation of God's
love, or its work, that is not the whole of the revelation.
The manifestation, the work even, needs exposition. The
deed needs to be carried home. The God in Christ needs
a prophet. God's son Jesus needed prophets, as God's son
Israel needed prophets, to expound his divine meaning
and purpose. The incarnation of God's love is too strange,
original and incredible; it needs to be interpreted by inspiration. Otherwise it would have been missed (as the disciples

during all Christ's life did miss it) and been lost. We do not call Christ himself inspired. That is a term too poor for him. Those were inspired in whom his spirit dwelt, his work went on, and his purpose wrought. The Christ needs the apostle, the preacher. The mediator upwards needs mediators downwards. For reasons I have gone into elsewhere, the divine doer of the divine work was somewhat reserved about the nature of that work. The task itself engrossed him. He could not talk much about it. The gospel he brought needed to become vocal by transmission through another experience as its prophet. And that other was the New Testament. *It is the inspired part of the revelation of which Christ was the incarnate redeeming agent.* It is not a direct document of Christ's biography, but of Christ's gospel, of Christ as preached. *It is a direct record, a precipitate if you will, not of Christ, but of the preaching about Christ which made the church.* It is of decisive consequence to realize this. *The Bible is not a voucher but a preacher.* The tradition of Christ we owe to a company of preachers, not to a jury of historians. The very Gospels are not biographies so much as pamphlets in the service of the church and the interest of the gospel. The only historical Christ which even the Gospels allow us to see is not a great figure Boswellized, but the *preached* Christ, the risen Messiah of the apostolic inspiration and the church's first belief.* The Bible is more of a sermon than of a source in the rigid historical sense of that word.

---

*The gospels (I keep saying) are not primary documents proceeding from Christ's hand. Nor can we be quite sure how far they come directly from apostles or even eye-witnesses. But I am referred to the preface of Luke. But it will be remembered that the author himself describes Luke in the preface to Acts as a treatise. Luke founded his account on sources but he is not himself a source in the same sense as his materials were. What he wrote is not a source but a history. He selected from sources on a certain principle, and treated them from a certain point of view—the view point of the risen, exalted, preached Christ as Savior.

The story was history with a drift, seeking a verdict; it was history made preacher. Something else than sequence guided the selection of incidents. *It is a story on a theme,* a story with a purpose. It is inferior as art but mighty as action. The writers are evangelists in the sense of gospellers. "These things are written that ye might believe that Jesus is Messiah, the Son of God; and that believing ye might have life through His name" (John 20:31). The object is life, not proof. These gospels are homiletic biographies, not psychological. They were not compiled on what we should call critical principles, but on evangelical principles—to assist the gospel. The evangelist with his narrative was but an acolyte of the apostle with his gospel. It is only thus that we can explain the fact that no apostle wrote a gospel, with the possible exception of John, who wrote expressly for a theology. They were too much absorbed in the gospel to write gospels for what they deemed but a short-lived world.

V.

The New Testament, then, is a record not directly of Christ but of the thing preached about Christ by those whose preaching made the church; and made historic Christianity. *You can of course say, if you like, that they misapprehended Christ,* that, led by the rabbinic Paul, they squeezed him into Jewish molds, and lost the real human, saintly Christ in a theological. You can say that, but what means have you to prove it? You are entirely dependent on the apostolic, the evangelical, the large Pauline version of Christ, whether in gospel or epistle. Paul preached what he had from the text he received from the church, "that Christ died for our sins according to the Scriptures." That links his gospel both to the other apostles and to the Old Testament. Every one of the Gospels is written in that interest of saving grace. What they go into is not a character, not an ethic,

nor a dogma, but a Savior. Whether you think they agree
in every point with the epistles or not, they are there not
as mere memorabilia for the curious but as edification for
the converted, not to save but to confirm the saved. They
all set forth not a humanist Christ, sweet, sage, and influ-
ential, but one whose main and crowning function was to
die for our sins according to older Scriptures. Is it not a most
singular thing that there is no indication in the whole New
Testament of an apostolic sermon with a saying of Christ for
a text? And the kingdom, which fills the Gospels, does not
appear in the epistles. What does that mean? It means that
the form and particulars of Christ's precious teaching were
not the staple of their message, not its starting point. These
precious details were all fused up in the still more precious
gospel in which Christ himself culminated through the cross.

Consider: *What were the apostles working with before
there was a New Testament and while they were making
the church?* It was with a message, a gospel, fact and act
of God through Christ, an achieved deliverance, a historic
redemption, crowning the long series of revelations and
deliverances which were at once the salvation and the
perdition of Israel. What was the great appalling thing
revealed to Paul in his conversion? Not the miracle of a
dead prophet's resuscitation. Not the idea of redemption.
That had long been the common burden of Israel, and it
was the source of all his zealotry. Like all earnest Jews he
was waiting for that consolation of Israel. But it was this
that staggered him—that the redemption was come and
gone. It was past and at work. That was for Paul "the power
of Christ's resurrection," the tremendous shattering, re-creat-
ing effect of it. The great thing to be done was already done.
God's redemption was not a hope now but a fact—and a
damnation. The Christians had a gospel and not a propa-
ganda, not a program, not a movement—merely a mighty
gospel. They had no book but the Old Testament, no system

of doctrine, no institution. All these were to be made. What they had was what they called the κήρυγμα, with all its foolishness (1 Cor. 1:21, where we hear of the scandal of the cross, the absurdity of what was preached, not of preaching as an institution). *The gospel was an experienced fact, a free and living word long before it was a fixed and written word.* This is the manner of revelation. The inspired thing is not a book but a man. It was so first of all in the Old Testament. The prophets also first experienced their gospel, then spoke or acted it. Only as an afterthought did they write it. The written form might be but a collection of their edited remains. The New Testament was the unfolding of this gospel; but it was an unfolding due to the free growth and power of God's saving act in the experience of certain men, and not to their examination of it and their conclusions. They were made by it rather than convinced. They were not students, critics of the gospel, but its glorious captives and alert hierophants. The gospel prolonged itself in them. That was the spirit's work. It was only at the call of certain providential junctures that what saved them made them write. It was "occasional" writing. It was not due to an academic resolution to discuss or celebrate what saved them. They did not "demonstrate." The gospel worked in them mightily to will and do, to preach and write in a practical context. Their writing was their work running over. Christ and *his* work energized in *their lives.*

The apostles, and especially Paul, *form an essential part of Christ's revelation of God's grace.* He represents grace as incarnate, they as inspired. He is epic, they are lyric. The same Christ reveals in them from heaven the redemption he wrought on earth. He prolongs his own action in them. He unfolds his finished work. They make explicit his mind about his own work. And through them he reveals this revelation in a way limited on one side by their personality, but on the other released from some of the bonds and

silences of his earthly humiliation. We have no evidence
that the *explicit* conception by the earthly Jesus of his own
work was all that appears in the epistles. It was in Paul and
his fellows that its nature became explicit, as it has become
still more explicit in successors of Paul, like the Reformers.
It was in these that the *mind* of Jesus came to itself for us
in history. It unfolded like a seed in the warm medium of
the apostolic soul. It was the Lord the Spirit speaking of
himself in the inspiration of the apostles, and speaking *to us*
more directly than the Gospels do. Like the prophetic books
in the Old Testament, the epistles are the authentic writings
of the inspired. They are not once removed, like the Gospels
or the Old Testament histories. They are not editorial, but
creative. They are evidence at first hand. They make a
critical starting point, and not only a critical, but an evangelical. They give the key to the Gospels, just as the prophets
in our new light form the basis for the interpretation and
the evangelical interpretation of Old Testament history. *The
epistles are essential, nay, normative, to the Gospels.* They
are not by-products. I do not wonder that Luther laid more
stress on them. Protestantism always must, for its life and
Christian promise. It is not Paul who speaks, but the Christ
living in him. (We discount, of course, what is plainly contemporary in Paul, or idiosyncratic.) There is, therefore, an
authority in the theology of the epistles which is in some
ways greater than we have in the Gospels as Gospels, as
writings, apart from the personality of Christ. There is more
inspiration in a creative Paul than in a compiling evangelist. In the Gospels Christ appears as acting, in the epistles the same Christ interprets his own action. And both
the manifestation and the inspiration are necessary for the
fulness of revelation as redemption, for its effect as a revelation *to us.*

We must not sharply contrast Paul and Christ. We cannot,
as I have said. *All we possess is the evangelical Christ com-*

mon to Paul, the other apostles, and the first church. We can compare the epistles and the Gospels. Their view point is the same—the gospel. They ply the same Christ the Savior. But the service of the evangelists is supplementary to that of Paul. They sustain the gospel he preaches. They, too, are preachers, but in a diaconal way. The gospel story but serves the gospel power, and the narrative is there to confirm the principle which the preaching reveals.

If this be so, then the most precious thing in Christ for the church is not his life story but his deed of gospel. It is not his teaching, not his personal influence, but his redemption. *It is a theological gospel, but it is not authoritative as dogma, but as revelation, as redemptive action.* It is the gospel, not in an exact theology, but in a theology of glow, and power, and range. It is this gospel that has made the New Testament. What inspired the apostles was not Christ's legacy of teaching about God or grace; it was grace itself, as the large burden of his life, moving onward and upward to the death and resurrection which fixed him as the Son of God in power. All this they found to be the agent of God's ancient purpose, and the gathering up for the world and for eternity of his gracious and active process of deliverance for Israel. What mastered and moved them for good and all in Christ was not mere personal affection, not appreciation of his discourse, nor the sense of his human kindness. These failed, and they left him and fled. What was authoritative for them at last was that in his cross they came to recognize the fulfillment of the ancient promise, the culmination of the long grace and the manifold redemption which was the burden of all Israel's history, the soul of its Scripture, and the world-purpose of its God.

VI.

That this is the true relation of the gospel to the Bible is shown by the case of Jesus himself. His Bible was the Old Testament. It had more influence on him at the center of his task than the contemporary Judaism, which affected but his form. *How did he use it?* That is a question that troubles some. He seems to shut the door in the face of modern scholarship by his uncritical use of the Old Testament. If he quotes Psalm 110 as David's, criticism (it is said) cannot go behind him. If he refers to Moses as the author of the Pentateuch, the scholars may spare their pains; the question is settled for them. And so people become entangled in Christ's relation to the Old Testament as literature, and they miss his relation to the Old Testament as revelation. They commit the error of rationalism. They put Christ at the mercy of critical considerations. They make them decisive instead of evangelical considerations. Let it be admitted that in all matters of science, literary or other, Jesus was the child of his time. He never claimed omniscience in that region. His reading of the Old Testament was certainly uncritical by the standards of our time and knowledge. In this respect he took it as he found it—like everybody round him. It was not his knowledge that was perfect. He found God in nature, but did he escape the current belief that the sun went round the earth? He read his time as no man did, but did he know times and seasons in the sense of days and dates? Did he not leave them to the Father, content not to know, and diviner in that precious ignorance of trust than in all knowledge? It was not his knowledge that was perfect, but his judgment. And on the composition of the Old Testament he never passed a judgment. It never occurred to him. If it had, it would not have interested him. Historic sequences were naught to him. What was infallible was not the views he inherited, but his grasp of the Father and the Father's purpose in him. It was in regard to his own work and gospel that he could not err. And no contemporary errors as to nature or the past affect the truth of his witness to God, or the power of his gracious saving work for man.

How then did Christ use his Bible? For we cannot be
wrong if we use ours in the same central way. *He used it as
a means of grace, not as a manual of Hebrew or other history.* His business was not to revise the story of the past or
disentangle origins, but to reveal and effect the historic
grace of God. He used his Bible as an organ of revelation,
not of information, for religion and not science—not even
for scientific religion. He found in it the long purpose and
deep scope of God's salvation, his many words and deeds of
redemption in the experience of the chosen race. He cared
nothing for the Bible as the expression of men's ideas of
God. He prized it wholly as the revelation of God's gracious
dealings with men. He cared for events only as they yielded
his Father's grace. He belonged to a race which was not
made like other races by an idea of God, but by God's
revelations and rescues. "I am the Lord thy God that
brought thee out of the land of Egypt, out of the house of
bondage." He did not teach us ideas of God. He was not
a sententious sage, full of wise saws or modern instances.
He did not move about dropping apophthegms as he made
them. He does not even tell us "God is love." It is an apostle
that does that. But he loves the love of God into us. He
reveals in act and fact a loving God.

> Sprich mir, wie redet Liebe?
> "Sie redet nicht, sie liebt."

> And, tell me, what does Love say?
> "Love doesn't say—it loves."

He saw the loving God in nature and in history; and within
history it was not in what men thought but in what God had
done. What he saw was the whole movement of the Old
Testament rather than its pragmatic detail. He dwelt loving-
ly indeed on many a gracious passage, but he found himself
in the total witness of Israel's history as shaped by grace.
*He cared little for what our scholars expound—the religion
of Israel.* His work is unaffected by any theories about the

Levitical sacrifices. What he lived on was God's action in his seers, God's redemption in his mighty deeds, as it rises through the religion of Israel, yea, breaks through it, shakes itself clear even of its better forms, and translates it always to a higher plane. What he found was not the prophets' thoughts of God, but God's action in Israel by prophet, priest, or king, God's invasion of them and their race by words and deeds of gracious power. It was the reality of God's action on the soul, and in the soul, and for the soul. Above all, it was the exercise and the growth of God's messianic purpose with the people, and through them on the whole race. It was in a messianic God that he found himself, and found himself God's Messiah-Son. Abraham! "Before Abraham was I am." If Abraham ceased would he? And he grasped what his whole age was blind to, the Old Testament witness, deep in its spirit, to a Messiah of the cross. In a word, *the torch he carried through the Old Testament was the gospel of grace.* He read his Bible not critically, but religiously. He read it with the eyes of faith, not of science; and he found in it not the making of history by men, but the saving of history by God.

That is to say *he read his Bible as a whole.* For he was its whole. And he lived on its gospel as a whole. Take the parables for an illustration. The chief spoken revelation of God is in the parables of Christ. What is the true principle of interpreting the parables? It is to treat each as the vesture of one central idea for whose sake it is there. We refuse to be entangled in the suggestiveness of details, as if it were allegories that Christ uttered. So it is with the verbal revelation of God altogether, the Bible. All its vast variety is there for one central theme and one vital purpose, to which details may sit loose. It was so, I say, that Christ read his Scriptures. And it is only when we read the Bible in this way, as a whole, that we realize that it is not there for its own sake, or for the sake of historical knowledge, but for the sake of the evangelical purpose and work of God. We do not read our Bible as Christ did if we dissect out portions of it as the Word of God and reject portions that are not. I do not say that that is forbidden. I shall indicate later that Christ did it on points outgrown. I have no objection to part with Leviticus, Esther, and Canticles from a gospel canon, however valuable they may be in a Hebrew library.* All I say is that the method of getting at the true Word of God in the Bible by dissection was not Christ's. And it is not decisive, and may be meticulous. The Bible within the Bible, the canon of the canon, is not to be dissected out, but to be distilled. What is most divine is not a section of it, but the spirit, the theme of it. God's great Word came less in fragments of writing than in his growing purpose through historic action and deeds of grace. The word of a prophet consisted in a kind of speech which was itself a deed, a practical revelation, relevant to the hour, of God's power, purpose, righteousness, judgment, mercy, and redemption.

VII.

It seems all but impossible to get out of the popular mind the idea that faith is faith in statements, and that the Bible is a compendium of truths about God, or a correct chronicle (or forecast) of history, Hebrew, Christian or cosmic. Almost all the uproar made against scientific criticism belongs to one or other of these irreligious positions. For it is irreligious to debase the Bible, the book of faith, to a repertory of truths, or a series of annals. It is irreligious to stake the divine value of Christ on the reality of pre-historic characters in Hebrew history, on the authorship of a Psalm, or

---

*While it may be granted that there are books in the canon that we could now spare, it ought to be owned also that there is no book known to us outside the canon that ought to be in a Bible whose note is redemption. We have nothing to do really with apostolic or non-apostolic distinctions, but only with books that carry the gospel note, whatever their origin.

the tracing of the atonement in Numbers. There are few perils to the Bible worse than the ill-tempered champions of late Protestant orthodoxy who pose as the monopolists and saviors of the gospel. "A traditional biblicism, hurled whole and harsh at the heads of those who read the book otherwise, is not faith in God's Word." The unity of the Bible is a living, growing, suffusing unity. It is the unity of a body with a quick and mighty spirit. It is a unity that may come home through much defect and loss in its body. A great conqueror may have but one eye or one arm. There are women whose every feature is wrong, more or less, but they bring all men to their feet.

> Faults she had once as she learned to run and tumbled:
>   Faults of feature some see, beauty not complete.
> Yet, good people, beauty that makes holy
>   Earth and air *may* have faults from head to feet.

The mighty and glorious gospel can speak freely from a vulnerable scripture canon. The canon, which is, so to say, the physical base of the gospel, may contain elements as superfluous as the appendix, or it may have a part amputated. The unity of the Bible is organic, total, vital, evangelical; it is not merely harmonious, balanced, statuesque. It is not the form of symmetry but the spirit of reconciliation. Strike a fragment from a statue and you ruin it. Its unity is mere symmetry, of the kind that is ruined so. But the unity of the Bible is like the unity of nature. It has a living power always to repair loss and transcend lesion. *The Bible unity is given it by the unity of a historic gospel, developing, dominant, but not detailed.* It transcends the vicissitudes of time, the dislocations of history, the frailties even of prophets and their proofs, and the infidelity of the chosen race. This is the unity that Christ found and answered in *his* Bible. His mastery of his Bible is not shown so much in his readiness with it as in his insight into it. It is not borne in on us by the command of it he showed in his irresistible dialectic with the Pharisees upon points; it appears rather in his grasp of its one historic grace; not in his ready wit with it but in the fact that he found himself to be the true Lord and unity of Bible, Temple, Sabbath and Israel. *If we are to take the Bible as Christ did we may not feel compelled to take the whole Bible, but we must take the Bible as a whole.*

But we shall be told that that gives us leave still to pick and choose according to some fantastic inner light, some extravagant and perhaps heartless scholarship, some individual verdict of the Christian conscience. Not at all. All these things, even the inner light, come to the Bible from without, like its detailed infallibility (which is a rationalist importation). But *the Christian key to the Bible, and its authority, is within itself.* It is the thing that produced it, the thing it exists for, wherewith it is in travail, the thing that makes Jesus to be Christ. It is the regnant gospel of a gracious God as moral redeemer. This mighty word uses the text of the Bible simply as we use the elements in communion, as sacred but not sacrosanct. The concern of some scrupulists about the detail of our great sacramental Scripture is quite parallel to the meticulous care by other scrupulists about the crumbs of the consecrated bread, or the dregs of the wine. The gospel is not a hard taskmaster; and as the Lord of the Bible it sits lightly on its throne, as lightly as only secure power can. We hamper the gospel if we case its subtle, lithe, and kingly spirit in a coat of literary mail. *The unity and power of the Bible is sacramental, it is not mechanical.* It is dynamic and not documentary. Faith in it is something more than the historic sense. And the water of life issues from it none the less mightily because the orifice may be cracked or broken. The very force of the water did that, as the spirit rent prophet and apostle, as we may enter the kingdom of heaven maimed.

I read the story of the father who petitions Christ to heal

his son. I seize the answer of the Lord, "I will come down and heal him." The words are life to my sick self. I care little for them as an historic incident of the long past, an element in the discussion of miracles. They do not serve their divinest purpose till they come to me as they came to the father. They come with a promise here and now. They are to me the words of the Savior himself from heaven. And upon them he rises from his eternal throne, he takes his way through a lane of angels, archangels, the high heavenly host and the glorious company of the saints. These congenial souls keep him not, and these connate scenes do not detain him. But on the wings of that word he moves from the midst of complete obedience, spiritual love, and perfect praise, restless in search of me—me sick, falling, lost, desperate. He comes, and he finds me and heals me in these words of gospel. I do not ask the critics for assurance that the incident took place exactly as recorded. I will talk of that when I am healed. It is a question for those who are framing a biography of Christ, or discussing the matter of miracles. The gospel of the Christ does not make its crucial appeal to human healthy-mindedness. For me these words are more than historical, they are sacramental. They are a vehicle of the gospel. Historically they were never said to me. I was not in Christ's thought when he spoke them. I was not in his thought upon the cross. But by the witness of the spirit to my faith they come as if they were said now to no one else. They come to me as they are in God. And I live on them for long, and I wait by their hope, and in the strength of them go many nights and days till I come to another mount of God.

Or when I read "He loved me and gave himself for me," do I trouble (when these words are most precious to me) about their value as an index of Paul's religion, or their bearing on a theory of atonement? The gospel leaps out of the Bible and clasps me. Who shall separate me, with all my wretched schism, from Christ's love? I have a measure now for the whole of Scripture in the living word which that embedded phrase has brought home to redeem my soul. The Bible has done its great work, not as a document of history, but as a means of grace, as a servant of the gospel, lame, perhaps, and soiled, showing some signs of age, it may be, but perfectly faithful, competent and effectual always.

VIII.

And even if *my* faith were too poor to find in the Bible more than a witness to history, a document for the church, a record of religious ideas; if *I* read it only for its interest to the modern mind, or its contribution to a noble humanism; or if I do not read it at all, but pursue a feeble, fanciful, subjective kind of piety, all this and more does not affect the authority of that gospel which is the burden of the Bible whole. *For the gospel's last appeal is not to individual faith nor to groups, but to the faith of its other product, the church.* The Bible as a great whole appeals to faith as a great whole. Deep calls to deep. The gospel, whose revelation used up a long, eventful, national history, has also produced a history longer and more eventful still in the continuous faith of the whole church. The grace which speaks from sundry portions of the Bible in diverse ways speaks to a manifold sum of Christian experience in the church of all times and climes. There is not a church that has not spoiled its witness in the telling, but there is none that has not told it, and told it because it knew it. As it is too great a gospel to be perilled on a scriptural incident, text, or book, so it is too great to be measured by individual or sectarian response. That many find nothing in it means little when set against what has been found in it by the experience of such a church, and done through it by the church's faith.

The Bible, therefore, has to do not with a pictured Christ,

but with a preached Christ. It does not stretch a figure but proclaims a gospel. And even of that gospel it is not a mere report. It is much more than a record, document, or source of information even about the first preaching. *It preaches that preaching.* It prolongs it. It is a source of power as well as knowledge. It is a living source in the religious sense. It is not only produced by the gospel, it is a producing source in turn. *The Bible, as produced by the Word, becomes integral to the Word, and so in course a producer of the Word.* It generates the faith that generated it, and it sends forth by its preaching a company of preachers. Faith comes from the preaching (from the Bible, that is), and the preaching came from the gospel Word of God. The Bible, from the nature of its origin, can never cease to produce preaching and preachers. Preaching must always be the supreme concern of a church that gives the Bible its proper place for the gospel. And it has been noted that probably more converts have been made by preaching from the Bible than by direct reading of it. Only, the preachers must read it all the more, and habitually read it, and come to close quarters with it, and know where they are with it, and treat it as their chief means of grace, the constant source of their salvation, mission, and power. *Nocturna versate manu versate diurna.* If you would preach a classic gospel, give your nights and days, your heart and head, to converse with the Bible. Our fathers had much to say about the *efficacy and sufficiency of Scripture.* And this was what they meant, its power to be a sacrament of the Word and pass the church on from faith to faith; its power to be a producing source of the faith that produced it, to prolong the Word in which it arose, and speed the message to which it is hands and feet. *To this gospel, which is the living totality of the Bible, the great witness is the faith which is the living totality of the church.* If the gospel of Christ's grace is the one authority set up among men, the seat of that authority is the Bible, and the witness is the faithful church. But, as it is the God that sanctifies the temple and not the gold, so it is the authority that hallows its own seat and not the seat's pattern or structure. The king is king by something else than the art found in his throne. And the gospel is supreme, not because it comes by a perfect, infallible book or church, but because it is the historic advent of the Savior God to the church's experience and faith.

IX.

The Bible can never be detached from the gospel, though it must be distinguished from it. *It is detachment from the Bible that is the mark both of Romanism at one end and of the religiosity of the modern mind at the other.* To take the latter first. The modern man feeds his religious nature on philanthropy, literature, journalism, pious booklets and sentiments, and writings generally meant for reading and not study—and all at the cost of the Bible. This happens even with preachers, whose eloquence and sympathy may but poorly cover the nakedness of their exegesis. And as to Rome's similar relation to the Bible, let me mention this. The great antagonist of Luther has been Loyola. Jesuitry is the real Counter-Reformation. And the essential difference between the two causes is indicated from their start. Both Luther and Loyola were crushed at their outset by the mighty hand of God. But Luther found his release, gospel and commission in serious contact with the Bible; while Loyola found his in visions, voices and fantasies, not essentially different from the subjective aspirations and intuitions of the modern heart. It is a far cry from the fierce ascetic Loyola to Mark Rutherford. But they join deep in their mystic frame. And the visions of the Jesuit are as subjective as the intuitions of the literary humanist, or of the modern hero who is converted by falling in love, and sanctified by the angel in the house. It would be useful to draw out the subtle and startling affinities between Jesuitism and the modern mind, between Catholic modernism and Protestant. There is no future for a Protestantism which shall be neither ritual nor sentimental, except it be founded directly on the objectivity of the Bible, and know how to use it. It is the gospel alone that can teach Rome its place. No other church can cope with Rome. Only the gospel can, purified to the message of abounding grace. The critics help us in their way to that, and the theologians still more. They help us to the objective which is Rome's strength. An objective and positive gospel is the only safety of our too subjective and fumbling faith. And it is the authority which above all others we need today, and especially in our pulpits. There is much fraternity, but there is too little mastery.

X.

The questions about the Bible are giving much trouble that finds expression, but much more that finds none. They are the source of much uneasiness that is felt, and of much decay of spiritual life that is felt but in part. They produce, among thousands that have never seriously faced them, *a vague sense of insecurity about the Bible,* and of its uselessness to the lay reader in consequence. It not only ceases to be an authority, but it ceases to be a means of grace for the soul and of support for the spiritual life. It becomes more of a problem than a stay. I am speaking of the effect within the church, among Christian people, not among the public. Very likely there is more Bible reading in the churches than we think; but, for all that, there is less than there used to be, when there should have been more. There is too little to maintain independent spiritual conviction, and vigorous spiritual life. There is a good deal of religious toying with the Bible, but there is not much real acquaintance with it, and not nearly what there should be in the pulpit. I am afraid this tendency will grow as the results of criticism filter down. And is it not certain that a church where the Bible is not each member's manual in an intelligent way is doomed to spiritual decay? It is condemned to ineptitude against a church or ministry making exorbitant claims for itself.

Is it not certain, further, that *the exit from the difficulty* lies in the direction I have indicated? It cannot lie in the way of ignorant denunciation of critical scholarship or the denial of its right. That right is now secure, both for the Old Testament and New. You may challenge certain results, but its method is now beyond question. It was historical criticism that destroyed the mythical theory of the Gospels; it was not the scandalized resentment of mere orthodoxy. But what secures the right? The church's own security in the gospel. *Only the evangelical certainty of faith in grace can guarantee the freedom of theology and learning in the church.* The church can handle the Bible fairly and freely only through the conviction that Bible and church are both there at the disposal of the gospel they stand to preach. But the "church's own security in the gospel"! I know how that will sound to some. It will mean the soundness of the church's views on such questions as atonement, justification, and faith. It will mean evangelical orthodoxy. Alas, I am afraid evangelical orthodoxy has to answer for much decay in the gospel's power and welcome. That is not what I intend. The fallacy lies in *the ambiguity of the word gospel.* This means two things. It means the mighty saving act of God in Christ; and it means the news of that act by the word of apostolic men. It means, first, God's Word to man, not spoken but done, by a Savior who spoke very little of it, and less and less as he drew near the doing of it. It means:

> the matchless deed achieved,
> Determined, dared, and done.

And it means, secondly, man's word under the influence of that deed of God, its expansion, its reverberation, so to say, in the souls it saved and inspired. It means the church's preaching of God's mighty work. We have thus the church's gospel of God's gospel. It is like the distinction between history and a history. The Bible is a living history of God's history in man. The one is not the other. The first draws all its value from the second. But the second without the first would be unknown. That preaching, that Bible which I call the precipitate of the first preaching of the apostles, has no other object than this, to be the sacramental channel of the power of God's redeeming deed. When I speak of the church's own security in the gospel I do not use the word gospel in the secondary sense. I do not mean the church's self-complacency with the way she has long delivered the message. That is the sign of a church dead and done with. And it is the badge of several churches. But I mean her sole and central confidence and obedience towards *God's act* of saving grace in Christ. Our security in the gospel is not our certainty of an evangelical creed, but our confidence in God's saving Son and grace. *That is really the one article of the Christian creed, God's grace redeeming from guilt in Christ.* And the response to it is the living, saving faith that alone makes a church a church. From this teeming center of Christian life there issues endless power and its endless freedom of thought and life, especially in regard to the letter and form of the Bible.

XI.

We have but one great sacrament. It is God's redeeming Word in Christ's cross. In this sacrament the Bible as a book takes the place of the elements. It is not the Bible that contains God's Word so much as God's Word that contains the Bible. These elements are involved in the sacrament, but they do not make its center of gravity. I have alluded to this aspect of the matter already; let me develop it. For us Protestants at least the virtue of the elements in a sacrament is quite independent of their chemical structure. We do not believe in transubstantiation. The power would come to faith were the elements water and fruit just as surely as by bread and wine. And it is just as great whatever our views may be of their composition, or if we have none. Now the Bible is the element which mediates the one great sacrament—the historic grace of God in Christ. And the structure, the chemistry, of the Bible is a secondary matter in regard to the communication of that grace. So long as it gives free course to God's gospel we may reach very new and strange conclusions as to items in it, the order of it, and the way it came to exist. The question is not of the integrity of the Bible, but of its efficacy for grace, its sufficiency for salvation, just as the question is not as to the punctilio of the ritual in the sacrament, but as to its blessing for living faith. *To stake the gospel upon the absolute accuracy of the traditional view of the Bible, its inerrancy, or its authorship by apostles, is just to commit, in a Protestant form, the Roman error of staking the sacrament on the correctitude of its ritual or the ordination of its priest.* Both the Bible and the church are living eucharistic things. But they draw their life solely from God's Word and act of institution in the cross, and from the spirit that proceeds from that God and gospel there. God gives his Word a body as he will, and he keeps giving that body, and keeps it fit for the purpose of grace at a given time. He has continually revised and readjusted the form of his church. There is not a church that exactly reproduces the primitive Christian community. Shall we be startled if the same is true of the Bible and its form? We do not want in the case of the church to restore the primitive form (or absence) of organization. We want to regain the first fine volume of faith and love through any church form that in our Christian judgment of the situation serves that end. And so with the Bible. We are not absolutely wedded to the views either of the apostles about the Old Testament or of the fathers about the New. It is the power, the efficacy, the sufficiency of the Bible for the uses of grace that is our grand concern, because that was the purpose which called the Bible into being as a whole. We are paying a very heavy penalty for using the Bible for texts and in sections. We have come to treat it in an atomistic instead of an organic way. The churches have almost lost the sense of its books as wholes, and of the book itself as a living whole submerging parts archaic or otiose. And yet it is there, in its corporate unity of grace, that the Bible's real power lies. There is its solidarity. We have lost our center of authority because we *would* construe the seat of authority as a document, a charter, a protocol, either for history or for orthodoxy, instead of a throne from which the charter issues and whose behests it serves. I would not insist on textual preaching if we had evangelical. I would not require the preacher to start from a verse, or a passage, or a creed, if he expound the great gospel and true creed of faith, with any amount of scope in its treatment that seems to him to light it up and carry it home.

XII.

The charter of the church is not the Bible but the redemption. The prophets repeatedly forced the church of Israel back on the great redemption from Egypt which gave the nation its fontal call. It was by his grasp of redemption that Athanasius saved the church in his day; his metaphysics being but the dialect of the day. And it was the same with Luther. The church's charter is a deed, not in the sense of a document but of an act of power reflected in the document. It is the power of God today in all the

churches with all their errors. It is a power which has sur-
vived ages when the Bible was much in abeyance, as in the
medieval church. It is a power which has dragged the Bible
from neglect, and set it on high again as the gospel's candle-
stick and the gospel's pulpit. But the Bible can never be the
surrogate of the gospel. The letter of the trust deed should
never submerge the bequeathing purpose it conveys. That
is the paganism of law which a law-church has drained of
the gospel and starved of intelligence. We never do the
Bible more honor than when it makes us forget we are
reading a book, and makes us sure we are communing with
a Savior. Secure in the gospel of God, we can take our true,
free attitude to its preaching by men, even by apostles. We
cannot do without their word. A revelation without historic
facts or personalities is no Christian, no real revelation. But
we may weigh by their theme their arguments and their
story, secure in our inheritance of grace by that word, in
which they stood. They have not dominion over our faith,
but they are helpers of our joy. There are sections of the
Bible which are so unintelligible to many of the best Christians that for them they might as well not exist. There are
facts that do not appeal to them, and are not used now,
however useful once. It looks as if our Lord himself exercised this spiritual selection on his Old Testament. There
were parts he found to have had their value only for their
own passing time. "Ye have heard—but I say." Would it be
fatal to the manner of his gospel to find that there were
similar parts for us even in the New Testament? But, you
say, if criticism reduce Christ's "reliable sayings to half a
dozen"! Well, that does not make critical scholarship anti-
Christian. It only rouses other critics and scholars to correct
such one-sided criticism, criticism where the scholar's memory has crushed his judgment, criticism with more pedantry
than historic sense, and without the sense of the gospel.
And it also warns us off the fatal error of interpreting the

work of Christ by his teaching instead of his teaching by his work. May we not select from among Christ's words as he selected from among those of the prophets? Surely. The evangelists did. And of those they give they nowhere state that it is a verbatim report exactly as it left his lips. Nor were all his precepts meant by himself to be perennial. Surely we may and must discriminate and exercise a critical selection. But by what clue? Let us use the supreme principle supremely. *Those words of Christ are prime revelation to us, and of first obligation, which carry home to us the saving grace incarnate in his person and mission.* The Holy Spirit which illuminates the Bible is the spirit which proceeds from the cross, the spirit which made Paul, who was made by the Christ not only as he lived, but chiefly as he died and lives for ever the Son of God with power. It is atoning grace that is our sanctification.

And I say all this with a deep sense of both *curiosa felicitas* of the phrase of Scripture which made its verbal inspiration so plausible, and of that searching profundity which is in the teaching of Christ. I have felt, as every scriptural preacher must, the Bible's ἀνίριθμον γέλασμα and its πλούσιον βάθος, its endless charm and its wealthy depth.

XIII.

The Bible not only provides but compels its own criticism by the Holy Spirit. It carries not only its own standard but the untiring spirit which from age to age compels us to apply that standard. This evangelical criticism is the most constructive of all. It is the kind of criticism which is a perpetual self-preservative. *There is no diviner feature of the gospel than its self-preservative power in history by self-correction and self-recovery.* The Reformation is the most striking illustration of this action of the spirit, which has been active in all ages in the church, though not successful

in all. It is the correction, the sanctification of faith by
faith, the reform of religion by religion, the re-reading of
the Bible by the gospel. What will remain of the Bible is
whatever is essential to the gospel. In the Reformation the
gospel test was applied by the spirit to the church. Today
we apply it by the same spirit to its other vassal the Bible.
We hear of the witness of the monuments to the Bible. But
the great ancient monument that verifies the Bible is the
cross, which stands in the Bible's own territory. The one
criticism which is adequately just to the Bible is this, the
Bible's inner self and final purpose of grace. Amidst all readjustments and dissolutions this must emerge freer and
ampler than ever. The great test of a religion must be religious, after all.

The public mind is far too much and too ignorantly occupied with the higher criticism, and far too little, too faith-
lessly, with the highest. And *the higher criticism itself has
gone too far alone.* I mean without the stamp and help of
the highest. It has in quarters lost itself in literary acumen
and philological detail. It is passing into a μεριμνοφροντιστήριον.
In the German laboratories they split documents as minutely
as the scholastics used to split hairs in dialectic, or the
Puritans in the divisions of their preaching. Indeed, the
situation is reproducing the feature that marked the downfall of scholasticism, Catholic or Protestant—the extreme
insulation of a method useful in its place. Now, as then, the
ruling scientific method breaks down of its own extravagant
ingenuity and untempered acumen. When the Reformation
came it applied religious criticism to religion. It rediscovered
the Bible by means of that gospel which made it challenge
the church. And today we carry the work on. The Reformation is reforming itself. It is in much need of reformation.
In a century after its origin it had sunk to a new scholasticism. Orthodoxy took the place of faith for the church, and
inerrancy was inflicted more severely on the Bible. Powerful

intellects went to work to systematize the great data of the Lutheran age. And it is this hard, keen theologizing, and not the large Reformation thought, that survives in much popular orthodoxy of a metallic sort today. The mighty stream was diverted into a thousand dialectic rills, and its old power was lost accordingly. A like thing has happened more recently to the speculative movement in philosophy. The great idealist age has been frayed out into an immense variety of scientific specialisms. The left of the movement won the day, and it has broken up into so many runnels on the field of mind that it can drive nothing. The meticulousness of orthodoxy on the one hand, and of criticism on the other, has joined with other influences in life, thought, and literature to make religion either vague or trivial. Criticism especially is now in danger of outstepping its high function, and, not being joined with faith, is moving to suicide after all it has so greatly done. It becomes the prey of the academic mind instead of the instrument of evangelical faith. The learned clergy becomes dons or humanists. The Bible scholars become pedants. They get out of touch with the public and with the gospel. The New Testament becomes an ancient text, dear to a scholarly church but ineffectual for the living Word. The plowers plow upon its back and long their furrows draw. They provoke among the Christian public a reaction which is ignorant enough, perhaps, but which means more than it knows, and much that the critics should heed. In their native land even the liberal theologians grow impatient of them, and the public still more.

XIV.

The great test, I have said, of a religion is religious. *Christianity will not stand or fall by its critical attitude to its documents, but by its faithful attitude to its gospel.* It is its self-criticism that will decide its fate, not the criticism of

the world, even of the learned world. Everything turns on
the criticism of faith by faith, on the final authority of the
gospel, standing at the altar and receiving the sound con-
tributions of the critical method. There are truths that need
to be restated in this light. But criticism alone cannot do
very much more. It has prepared for a higher reconstruction which is overdue, the serious use of a revised Bible for
its revising gospel. For instance, we do not need further
histories of Israel, nor histories of the religion of Israel.
That is not what the church needs at least. What we need
from a scholar equipped with the soundest results, however
new, is what Jonathan Edwards gave his day, a history of
redemption, a history of the revelation always welling up
through the religion of Israel and of Christendom at once
purifying it and condemning it. In the Old Testament we
have a blended record both of Israel's religion and of God's
revelation. In the New Testament there are traces of similar
action. And it is very striking in the history of Europe, in
the struggle (and infection) of Catholicism with the indige-
nous paganisms. We need now that the revelation which is
vital to the church that prolongs the gospel be disentangled
from the popular religion, ancient or modern, and shown on
its conquering way.

XV.

We need, in a closing word, that the free churches
should do what they have not yet done, that they should
really *face the spiritual situation created by the collapse of
biblical infallibility for those communities that have long
repudiated the final authority of the church.* To come to
terms with culture (in this sense of the word) is at least as
necessary for the churches in their action on society as to
come to an understanding with labor or the democracy. The
high church party began to do it in *Lux Mundi* by accept-

ing critical results in the strength of the church and sacraments. To us that way is closed. But the one true and living way is open. It is the way of the gospel and the sole authority of its grace, which is now, since the Catholic reaction, the special charge of the free churches of this land.

2. The Distinctive Thing in Christian Experience

In this article of 1908 Forsyth describes Protestant theology as it rests on the Reformation and the Enlightenment (Illuminism). Forsyth agrees that there is a conflict between these mental worlds and claims that we have accepted much "which would have scared even the stout reformers." What is left is to believe *in* Christ, not *like* him. This is an ethical conviction dependent on the inner witness of the Holy Spirit. Historical documents and reliance on their sober and solemn repose is to find in the peace of God a deadening calm. Here on the scale of history the peace of God is a mighty confidence in Christ. "We may respond to a saint, but to Christ we belong."

In *The Principle of Authority* Forsyth relates that confidence as belief which wills to receive and obey. "A process of thought apart from an act of will would bring us to no conclusion, to nothing that could be called certainty." By such an act of will the Christian is transformed into a believer.

❖   ❖   ❖

From the *Hibbert Journal*
VI (1908)

I.

Our present Protestantism is historically composed from the union of two streams, which take their rise in two different sources. They still flow alongside with a fusion so far very incomplete, and they react on each other with an amount of irritation somewhat inexplicable till we perceive that the streams are two, distinct in their origin and direction. They are the Reformation and the Illumination: the Reformation from the sixteenth century, and the diversified movement which marked the eighteenth century, and which is compendiously known as the Illumination or the *Aufklärung.* They are the old Protestantism and the new—the one resting on the objectivity of a given revelation, the other on the subjectivity of human nature or thought; the one finding its standard in a divine intervention, the other in immanent human reason more or less generously construed; the one emphasizing a divine redemption, the other human goodness and its substantial sufficiency. The face of the one movement is towards the church and the Bible, the face of the other is towards civilization and culture. The one falls back upon historic humanity, upon the history and the revelation there; the other on intrinsic humanity and the revelation there. It is a distinction much more penetrating than the somewhat vulgar antithesis of orthodoxy and heterodoxy. It is not so much two theologies as two methods—if not two religions. And neither is pure. The one, the Reformation stream, carries down with it much of the debris of medieval doctrine; because at its source, in the monk Luther, it was

---

*For a full account of the situation we should really have to recognize three streams. We should have to distinguish within Protestantism the old objective tendency, resting on history as the authoritative source (in the Bible), and the newer subjective tendency, resting on Christian experience, originating in Anabaptism, revised in pietism, and rewritten in Schleiermacher. The one represents classic Protestantism, the other romantic. But the present purpose it will be better to confine our attention mainly to the two currents named in the text. Of course, the subjectivity of human nature, which I mention immediately, becomes in pietism, the subjectivity of Christianized human nature.

mainly a religious and ethical change rather than a theological. The other, the Illumination, carries with it much of
the pagan debris of the older Renaissance and of classic
ambiguity; since its element was not so much religion as
thought, and its achievement is not faith but culture, and
especially science. It was really directed at first not against
religion, but against what it thought a false basis of religion.
It sought to replace imagination by induction as the foundation of our conception of the world. It asserted the intrinsic divinity of nature, and it would make the spiritual life
but the highest of natural phenomena. While, therefore,
the direct legacy of the Reformation laid fundamental stress
upon the sense of guilt, and the action of grace, the legacy
of the Illumination laid stress on native goodness, the sense
of rational sympathy, and the sufficiency of human love
spiritualized. For the one, man was the lost thing in the
universe, and the greatness of his ruin was the index of the
dignity of his nature; for the other, man was the one saving
thing in the universe, and the greatness of his success in
subduing the world to his thought and will was the badge
of his heroic divinity, soiled perhaps, but indelible. The one
lived by redemption and regeneration, the other by evolution and education. For the one forgiveness was essential,
and it was identical with the new eternal life; it put life on
a quite new track, it was a redemption, a revolution. For
the other forgiveness was incidental, and simply removed
obstacles or redressed lapses in man's developing career;
it put the train on the old track, after some derailment by
accident, or some loop-line by error. It was a restoration.
The one cultivated theology and sanctity, the other science
and sentiment, criticism and romance. The one saw the new
Jerusalem descending from God, the other saw it rise "like
an exhalation" from earth. The heaven of the one was in
the blue sky, for the other it was in the growing grass. For

the one the great matter was God's transcendence over the world, for the other it was his immanence in it. The one degenerated to deism, the other to pantheism. For the one the incarnation was nothing but miracle, inexplicable but sure; for the other it was nothing but universal immanence. For the one redemption was an interference, for the other it was an evolution. For the one Christ was absolute, for the other he was but relative to the history from which he arose. For the one he closes the old series totally in the new creation of another, for the other he but mightily prolongs it. In the one case we believe *in* Christ, in the other we believe *like* Christ. For the one Christ is the object of our faith, for the other he is the captain of our faith, its greatest instance. In the one we trust our whole selves to Christ for ever, in the other we imitate him. In the one he is our God, in the other our brother. It is well that the issue should be clear, if our choice is to be as intelligent and effectual as a faith should be.

These are the two streams whose junction forms current Protestantism, and can you wonder that the situation is complicated and even confused? We should trivialize the whole subject if we saw in the serious religious differences of the day no more than orthodoxy and heterodoxy—the propriety of certain individuals on the one hand, faced by the perversity of certain others on the other. The conflicting views of Messrs X and Y are but the points where old opposing forces for the moment emerge and meet.

And we must own each movement has its relative justification. The old Protestantism had come to have great need of the Illumination. It was becoming cumbrous, hard and shallow. It needed especially to be trimmed down and cleared up from the critical side of the Illumination, and to be deepened and humanized from its romantic side. In just the same way medievalism had called for the Renaissance.

But all the same it was not the Renaissance that really took Europe in hand at that crisis. It was no paganism that could save Europe for the true church, or the church for Christianity. That was done by the self-recuperative power of Christianity itself. It was done by the self-reformation of the church, by the restoration of faith, and not the renascence of culture. Remember, the Reformation was not something done *to* the church, but *by* it, and therefore by its faith. And so today it is not to the Illumination, it is not to any culture, theological aesthetic, or scientific, that we are to look for our salvation from the Protestant scholasticism which choked faith by orthodoxy in the seventeenth century and still survives in the popular levels. That deliverance can only come by a movement from the interior of faith itself. I know it would be untrue to say that all the liberalizing influence in the Protestantism of today is due to the direct action of the Reformation spirit of faith or religion. In so far as that liberality is a correction of our views about God in the cosmos, it is due quite as much, if not more, to the Illumination, which was quite independent of the reformers and rose rather from the philosophers. But the real matter is not the correction of views but the correction of real religion, of practical relations between God and the soul. And that is due, not to the action of either reason or romance, but to the renovation of faith by the piety and genius of men like Spener, Francke, Schleiermacher, and Wesley.*

It is not here a question whether each tendency must ban the other, for we need both; but it is a question which of them must be dominant for Christianity, and especially for original, essential Christianity. I mean for Christianity as first preached, the Christianity of the Bible and the apostle. In proportion as it ceases to be a κήρυγμα, Christianity ceases to be Christianity, whether it die in the direction of a sacra-

---

*I do not forget the influence of the romantic movement on Schleiermacher, but it was perhaps upon his weaker and less permanent side.

mentalism or a humanism. It seems to me that this is
constantly overlooked by the spokesmen of a Christianity
which is liberal or nothing. They become as much the
doctrinaire victims of a speculative theology as our fore-
fathers were the victims of an orthodox theology. The experimental gospel in each case ceases to be life, and evaporates
to a *caput mortuum* of certain views broad or narrow. I
read a criticism of a positive theologian by a liberal of the
academic stamp in which occurred this naive saying: "It
looks as if the problems of theology were here confused
with the practical declaration of the gospel by preacher or
pastor." There is not one of the apostles that would not be
hit by the remark. And it applies with even more force to
our Lord himself. Where are we to go for our Christian
theology except to their practical declaration of the gospel?
The New Testament is no collection of theological loci.
And how are we to test a theology at last but by its service
for the purpose of the gospel? Of course, if it is not a theology we are after but a theosophy, if our interest is in the
philosophy or psychology of religion as a product of the
human spirit, the case is altered. But with that the gospel
and the preacher have little directly to do. It is very interesting, but it is not vital. It belongs to the schools, to the interpretive efforts of man upon the world; it has little to do
with the church and its interpretive message of man's destiny and its gospel of God's reality in his redemptive work.

When the question is forced, therefore, whether the positive or the liberal movement must rule in a historic gospel,
we have no hesitation about our choice. We take the Reformation side of our Protestantism for a stand, and not the illu-
minationist. We may even go so far, when the issue is forced,
as to say that illuminationism or rationalism is not Protestantism. We find our charter in history, and not in human
nature; in the Word, and not the world. The seat of revelation is in the cross, and not in the heart. The precious thing

is something given, and not evolved. Our best goodness is presented to us rather than achieved by us. The kingdom of God is not a final goal, but an initial boon. You will say, perhaps, the one does not exclude the other. But for the practical issue on which all turns (except to a doctrinaire intellectualism), for the last reality, it is more true at this juncture to press the antithesis than to slur it. The gospel stands with the predominance of intervention, and it falls with the predominance of evolution. Grace is essentially miraculous. Christ is more precious to us by what distinguishes him from us than by what identifies him with us. The gospel turns entirely upon redemptive forgiveness; and if evolution explain all, there is no sin, and therefore no forgiveness. The gospel turns on the finality of Christ; but on an evolutionary idea there is no finality except at the close; it is therefore inaccessible, for the end is not yet. There can be no finality on that basis, in anyone who appeared in a middle point of the chain. So far, therefore, Christ is provisional and tentative till a greater arise. The positive gospel, we say, is the dominant thing by which modern thought must be gauged and its permanence tested. We may take from the modern mind and its results so much only as is compatible with a real, historic, redeeming, final gospel. That gospel is the preamble, and the subsequent clauses that contradict it must go out.

We shall not be foolish enough, sectarian enough, to make a sweeping condemnation of modern thought in advance. For one thing, it is very hard to know what is meant by it. Does it mean the mental world of Kant, and Goethe, and Browning, or of Spencer, Fiske, and James, or of Nietzsche, Tolstoi, and Ibsen? Because they are in many respects as incompatible with each other, and hated by each other, as they are opposed to evangelical Christianity. And, for another thing, we have already accepted many of the results of modern civilization. It has thrust back the frontier of the

church, and given a mandate to the state to take up province
after province which the church used to control in art,
science, philanthropy, education, and the like. Well, we
largely agree. We accept the emancipation of these from
religious dictation. Church discipline gives way to civic
rights and police protection. The number of public subjects
on which the preacher is entitled to a respectable opinion
grows fewer, while at the same time there are more aspects
than ever of his own subject opened to his study and demanding his official attention. We accept the modern repu-
diation of an external authority in the forms of belief and
uniformity of confession. We accept the essential inwardness
of faith even when we press its objective. We accept the
modern freedom of the individual. We accept the modern
passion for reality, which owes so much to science. We
accept the methods of the higher criticism, and only differ
as to its results. We accept the modern primacy of the moral,
and the modern view of a positive moral destiny for the
world. And we repudiate imagination, whether aesthetic
or speculative, as the ruling factor in the religious life. We
have assigned another place and function to the miraculous
in connection with faith. We accept the modern place
claimed for experience in connection with truth; we recognize that the real certainty of Christian truth can only come
with the experience of personal salvation. In these and other
respects we have already accepted much which would have
scared even the stout reformers.

II.

I would single out for particular stress the place now
given to experience in religion in consequence of the Reformation view of faith, cooperating with the inductive method
of science—our experience of Christ especially. What nature
is to science, that is Christ to positive faith. I would direct

notice to the form of the great issue presented in the question: Are we to believe *in* Christ or *like* Christ? Are we to trust ourselves to him, or to the type of religion he represents?

I am struck with the absence of any sign of an experience distinctively Christian in many of those who discuss the sanctuaries of the Christian faith—such as the nature of the cross, or of the self-consciousness of Christ. To them Christ's first relation is to human power, or love, and not to sin. They cultivate not trust in Christ, but the "religion of Jesus." We are driven from pillar to post, and left with no rest for the sole of our foot. Can we rest on the Gospels? No. Criticism will not allow that. Can we on the epistles? No. Protestantism will not allow that. It would be taking the external authority of an apostle for our base, and that ends in Rome. But is there no such thing any more as the *testimonium Sancti Spiritus?* No. These scholars, to judge from their writings alone, do not seem even so much as to have heard of a Holy Ghost. And they have a fatal dread of pietism, and methodism, and most forms of intensely personal evangelical faith. They are, like Haeckel, in their own way, the victims of an intellectualism which means spiritual atrophy to Christianity at last. No, they say, if you fall back on your experience, you may land anywhere.

But am I really forbidden to make any use of my personal experience of Christ for the purposes even of scientific theology? Should it make no difference to the evidence for Christ's resurrection that I have had personal dealings with the risen Christ as my Savior, nearer and dearer than my own flesh and blood? Is his personal gift of forgiveness to me, in the central experience of my life, of no value in settling the objective value of his cross and person? My personal contact with Christ, our commerce together, may I found nothing on these? "No," it is said, "nothing of scientific objective value. These experiences may be of great personal value to you, but they give you no warrant for stepping outside your own feelings. They may be useful illusions in their place, but you must outgrow them. You can never be quite sure that the Savior you meet is a personal reality. You can never make it certain to any that he is a continuous personality with the historic Jesus. And it is even laid upon us to make it doubtful for yourself." "In your so-called communion with Christ you have no more real right," we are told, "to build on the objective personal reality of your *vis à vis* than the Roman Catholic girl had to believe in the real presence and speech of the virgin at Lourdes. If it is Christ who visits you, it was the virgin that visited her. Of so little worth is the fact of the experience in vouching for the content of experience. If you commune with Christ, do not grind at those who traffic with the saints."

Now, might I have leave to say that I had to meet that problem for myself several years ago? And the answer I thought satisfactory was twofold. First, it was personal; second, it was historical.

I take the first first. There is, and can be, nothing so certain to me as that which is involved in the most crucial and classic experience of my moral self, my conscience, my real, surest me. A vision might be a phantom, and a colloquy an hallucination. But if I am not to be an absolute Pyrrhonist, doubt everything, and renounce my own reality, I must find my practical certainty in that which founds my moral life, and especially my new moral life. The test of all philosophy is ethical conviction. That is where we touch reality— in moral action, (God as spirit is God *in actu*), and especially in that action of the moral nature which renews it in Christ. Now, my contention is that my contact with Christ is not merely visionary, it is moral, personal and mutual. Nor is it merely personal, in the same sense in which I might have personal intercourse from time to time with a man in whom I am little concerned between whiles. Because what I have in Christ is not an impression, but a life change; not an impression of personal influence, which might evaporate, but a faith of central personal change. I do not merely feel changes; I am changed. Another becomes my moral life. He has done more than deeply influence me. He has possessed me. I am not his loyal subject, but his absolute property. I have rights against King Edward, however loyal I am, but against Christ I have none. He has not merely passed into my life as even a wife might do, but he has given me a new life, a new moral self, a new consciousness of moral reality. In him alone I have forgiveness, reconciliation, the grace of God and therefore the very God (since neither love nor grace is a mere attribute of God). There has been what I can only call a new creation, using the strongest word in my reach. I owe him my total self. He has not merely healed me, in passing, of an old trouble, but he has given me eternal life. He has not only impressed me as a vision might—even one projected from my own interior—but he has done a permanent work on me at my moral center. He has made a moral change in me which, for years and years, has worked outwards from the very core of my moral self, and subdued everything else to its obedience. In my inmost experience, tested by years of life, he has brought me God. It is not merely that he spoke to me of God or God's doings, but in him God directly spoke to me; and more, he did in me, and for me, the thing that only God's real presence could do. Who can forgive sin but God only, against whom it was done? Thus the real Catholic analogy to his action on me and in me is not visions of the virgin, or the ecstasies of saints, but it is the sacraments. In the Catholic view these are objective and effective upon the inmost substantial self; so is Christ objective, effective, creative, upon my moral, my real self, upon me as a conscience, on sinful me. He is the author not of my piety merely but of my regeneration. My experience of him is that of one who does a vital, revolutionary work in that moral region where the last certainly lies. And in that region it is an experience of a change so total that I could not bring it to pass by any resource of my own. Nor could any man effect it in me. And any faith I have at all is faith in Christ not merely as its content nor merely as its point of origin, but as its creator. The Christ I believe in I believe in as the creator of the belief, and not merely its object. I know him as the *author* as well as object of my faith. The great change was not a somersault I succeeded in turning, with some divine help; it was a revolution effected in me and by him. The very fact that in its nature it was forgiveness and regeneration makes it a moral certainty, the kind of certainty that rises from contact with my judge, with the last moral and personal reality, who has power even to break me, and with my redeemer, who has power to remake me as his own.

If certainty does not lie there, where can it be found in life? If he is not real, moral reality has no meaning. There are hallucinations in religious experience, but not here. They might be connected with the affections but not with the conscience at its one life-crisis. They might be as impressive as a *revenant,* but not creative, redemptive. If you claim the right to challenge the validity of my experience, you must do it on the ground of some experience surer, deeper, getting nearer moral reality than mine. What is it? Does the last criterion lie in sense, or even in thought? Is it not in conscience? If life at its center is moral, then the supreme certainty lies there. It must be associated, not with a feeling nor with a philosophic process, but with the last moral experience of life, which we find to be a life morally changed from the center and forever. To challenge that means rationalism, intellectualism, and the merest theos-

ophy. Do not forget that philosophy is but a method, while
faith, which is at the root of theology, presents us with a
new datum, a new reality.

You refuse the mere dictum of an apostle. But if we may
not rest upon the mere dictum of an apostle, may we not
upon our own repetition of the apostolic experience, the
experience which made them apostles? I say repetition, but
might I not say prolongation? We rest on our own participa-
tion in the ageless action of the same redemption in the
cross as changed them, after many waverings, for good and
all. Is it not the same act, the same spirit, the same real
personality acting on us both, in the same moral world?
And, expanding my own experience by the aid of theirs, may
I not say this: I am not saved by the apostle or his experience, nor by the church and its experience, but by what
saved the apostle and the church. When Christ did for me
what I have described, was it not the standing crisis of the
moral macrocosm acting in its triumphant way at the center
of my microcosm? Was not the moral crisis of the race's
destiny on Christ's cross not merely echoed but in some
sense re-enacted at my moral center, and the great conquest
reachieved on the outpost scale of my single crisis? The
experience has not only a moral nature, as a phase of conscience, but an objective moral content, as is shown by the
absolute rest and decisive finality of its moral effect in my
life and conduct. If it be not so, then we are asked to believe
that men can produce in themselves these changes which
permanently break the self in two, or can lift themselves
to eternal moral heights by their own waistband. But, if so,
what need is there for a God at all? Do not even the posi-
tivists likewise?

There is no *rational* certainty by which this *moral* certainty *could* be challenged; for there is no rational certainty
more sure, or so sure, and none that goes where this goes,
to the self-disposing centers of life. This moral certainty is

the truly rational certainty. Christ approves himself as a reality by his revolutionary causal creative action on that inmost reality whereby man is man. That center from which I *act* (and therefore am real) meets, in a way decisive for all life, with Christ in his act on the cross. If this contact represent no real activity on me, if it be but impressionist influence, then the whole and central activity of my life, whereby I confront it in kind, is unreal. If the Savior be unreal and my communion an unreality, a mere mystic or moody mingling of being, then there is no reality, and everything is dissolved into cloud and darkness and vapor of smoke.

I do not wish to say anything disrespectful of these academic critics to whom we owe so very much in the way of laboratory theology, but they are the second, not the first. A higher hand must make them mild. A deeper insight must enlarge their truth. And I much wish they had more of that ethical realism of Carlyle or Ibsen, only turning it upon the conscience at the cross. But so often (just as a vast memory may impair the power of judgment) you find the finest critical faculty, and the most powerful scholarly apparatus, conjoined with a moral nature singularly naive and beautifully simple and unequal to the actual world. Their experience of life and conscience has no record of lapse or shame. Their world is a study of still-life; it has not the drama, the fury, the pang, the tragedy, the crisis of the actual world at large, with its horrible guilt and its terror of judgment. It opens to them none of the crevasses where glow the nether fires. They inhabit, morally, the West End. They are in no touch with damned souls. They have lived in an unworldly purity, and have never been drawn from the jaws of hell, or taken from the fearful pit and its miry clay. They have been reared, many of them, in the sacred and pious atmosphere of the German manse, and cradled in the godliness of the most Christian of homes. The paradox is this, that if purity be the test of truth, and obedience the organ of theological knowledge, if that be the meaning of "will do, shall know" (as it is not), if they are as right in their views as they are of heart, then evangelical Christianity would be dying of its own moral success.

III.

The second part of my answer to the suggested analogy between communion with a saint and communion with Christ is this. It would enlarge what I have been saying to the scale of history. Christ has entered actual history, with piercing, crucial, moral effect, in a way the virgin never has, nor any saint. He has entered it not only profoundly, but centrally and creatively; she is adjutorial at most. By his effect upon human experience he created that church within which the worship and contact of the saints arose. The church arose as a product of something which Christ produced. And it is not only the effect of Christ on the church that I speak of, but, through the church, his effect on history at large. Christ affects the moral springs of history as no saint has done. They but color the stream; he struck from the rock. I make all allowance for the fact that, by the church's fault, he has affected history less than he might have done. But it remains true that all we have and hope in the new humanity owes to Christ what it owes to no other. And it owes it to a Christ felt and believed to be generically different from every rival or every believer. What we owe to Christendom, or to great Christians, they owe to a Christ who owed himself to no man. He has entered the history of the church at least as he has entered my history —not as the mere postulate, nor even as the spring, but as the creator of the new life, the new self, while he himself needed no new self or new life. I make all allowance for the reasonable results of historic criticism, yet he stands in history as a defined consciousness and a creative person, who is powerful not in the degree in which he is appreciated by our experience, but in a way which creates experience and which can only be appreciated by something greater than our experience—by our faith. We know him by faith to be much more than he has ever been to our experience. I know him, and the church knows him, as a person of infinite power to create fresh experience of himself. My contact with him by faith is continually deepening my experience of him. And as my experience deepens it brings home a Christ objective in history, and creative of the experience, and the life, and the deeds of a whole vast church meant, and moving, to subdue mankind not to itself, but to the faith of the gospel.

But how can an individual experience give an absolute truth? How can an experience (which is a thing personal to me in, say, my own forgiveness) assure me of the world? How can my experience, my forgiveness, assure me of the world's redemption? How can it assure me of the final and absolute establishment of the kingdom of God? I may experience my salvation, but how can I experience the salvation of the world—which is for all (and is so felt by some) a greater concern than their own?

The answer is this. My experienced salvation is not a passing impression but a life faith. It is not a subjective frame but an objective relation, and even transaction. The peace of God is not glassy calm but mighty confidence. My experience here is the consciousness not of an impression on me, but of an act in me, and by me. It is not an afferent but an efferent consciousness, as the psychologists would say, like the muscular sense, the sense not of rheumatism but of energy. And, to go on, it is the sense not only of myself as acting in the experience called faith, but it is the sense that that act is not perfectly spontaneous but evoked, nay, created by its content. And, still to go on, it is the sense that it is created by another and parent act—which is the one eternal decisive act of an eternal person saving a world. I am for-given and saved by an act which saves the world. For it not only gives me moral power to confront the whole world and surmount it, but it unites me in a new sympathy with all mankind, and it empowers me not only to face but to hail eternity. And this it does not for me, but for whosoever will. This is the report of my faith and of the church's faith upon the act to which it owes its own existence as an act. Is it amenable to unfaith? *Actor sequitur forum rei,* said Roman law. The venue of criticism is in the court of the challenged faith. That is, the true and fruitful criticism is that within the believing church. It is a part of that self-criticism of the church whose classic case is the Reformation.

What Christ has done for me has become possible only by what he did even more powerfully for others whose faith and experience have been deeper and richer than mine, but who reflect my experience all the same, even while they diversify and enlarge it mightily. Standing over my experi-ence is the experience of the whole evangelical succession. And standing over that is the historic fact of Christ's own person, and his consciousness of himself ("All things are delivered to me of the Father") as Lord of the world, Lord of nature in miracle, of the soul in redemption, and of the future in judgment. When I meet him in my inmost soul, I meet one whose own inmost soul felt itself to be that, and who has convinced the moral power of the race in the whole historic church that he *is* what he *knew* himself to be. And in that conviction the church has become the mightiest power that ever entered and changed the course of history from its moral center.

Our experience of Christ is therefore an absolutely dif-ferent thing from our experience of saint or virgin. In their case, granting it were actual, the visitation might be but my experience; in his case it is my faith, which concerns not a phase of me whereof I am conscious, but the whole of my moral self and destiny whereof I am but poorly conscious. We may respond to a saint, but to Christ we belong.

IV.

The third part of my answer would expand what I have touched on, a few words back, in regard to the consciousness of Christ.

I have referred to the individual experience, and to its expansion in the experience of the church. But is this enough to give us the reality of a supernatural (or rather a superhistoric) Christ? If it were, then we should be in this difficulty, that the experience of believers would be the seat of God's revelation to us. And fresh difficulties arise out of that. If it be so, then do we not give the church (as the collective experience) a prerogative which, even if it does not rise to the claim of Rome, yet puts the individual conscience too much at its mercy, and obtrudes the church between it and Christ? And, again, if it be so, what was the seat of God's revelation to the very first church of all, to the first believers with no church behind them? And what place is left for the Bible, the record, at all except a mere subsidiary one in support of the supreme experience of a church? Whereas the Bible, no less than the church, was a parallel result of the gospel, and part of the revelationary purpose of God. The gift of the spirit* to the apostles was not simply to confirm personal faith but to equip them efficiently for their apostolic, preaching, witnessing work.

We must pass within the circle of the first church's experience and testimony, and find a means of stepping off the last verge of its direct documentation on to sure moral ground where the documents cease. We must pass by faith

---

*The difficult question as to the relation between Christ and the spirit (especially for St. Paul) is too large for side treatment. I only note that our communion is not with the spirit, but in the spirit, with the Father and Son.

from the field of the first faith certificated in the documents to the historic reality behind the wall of documents, and within the ring fence of the testifying church.

And we are compelled to do so by the very nature of that faith and those documents themselves. If we are not to stultify the first church and all its history, we must recognize a point on which critics so antagonistic to each other as Schaeder and Lobstein agree,* that the gospel about Jesus in the first church truly reflected Jesus' gospel of himself, and grew inevitably out of it. We could not speak of Jesus with any respect if his influence not only could not protect his first followers from idolatry in placing him where they did—beside God in their worship—but actually promoted that idolatry. If *they* included Christ in his own gospel, then *he* did. It was not in the teeth of him that they made him an object of faith and worship along with the Father. They could never have treated him, those disciples who had been with him, in a way which would have horrified him as much as some apostles were horrified at the attempt to worship them at Lystra. If they found him Savior through death from sin, found him the Son of God and the eternal Christ, then he offered himself as such.

Accordingly the question becomes one of the interpretation of his self-consciousness as the Gospels offer it upon the whole. We are borne onward by the experience of the church upon the experience of Christ in so far as he revealed it. The church's first thought of him was substantially one with his own thought of himself. What was that? Was it a thought which placed him with men, facing God and moving towards God, or with God facing men and moving to them? Was he not always with men, but from beside God? Can our relation to him, if we take his construction of it, be parallel to our relation to any apostle, saint, virgin,

*See *Die christliche Welt,* 1907, No. 19, Sp. 529.

or hero? Into the self-consciousness of Christ I cannot here
go. I can only refer to all the passages of the Gospels which
have their focus in Matt. 11:25 ff.,* and which reveal the
sense of his complete mastery of the world of nature, of the
soul, and of the future. He forgave the soul and claimed
to judge it. He determined our eternal relation to God. And
he used nature at will for the supreme purposes of grace
and eternity.

But we must here take another step which replaces us
where we set out, though on a higher plain. This power of
which Jesus was so sure was not there simply to make a
vast and placid self-consciousness. He was not there simply
as a reservoir of moral power instead of its agent. If he
had the power it was not as a miser of power, to enjoy the
satisfaction of possessing it in self-poised and self-sufficient
reserve, not to be a quiescent character reposing in God.
He was there to exercise the power in historic action. And
as it was moral power, it could only go out in moral achievement. He was there for a task in which the whole of it should
be expended. He was there to do something which only
his power could do. If he had power more than all the
world's, it was to overcome the world in another than the
individualist and ascetic sense. It was to subdue it to himself. The Son was not only to affect it, but to regain it for
the Father. He was not simply to rule, but to redeem. He
was there for action; and it was action commensurate both
with his person, and with the world, and with the world's
moral extremity. He was there to do that which all the
accounts declare was done in the cross—to conquer for
mankind their eternal life. It was not simply to fill men's
souls at his as from a fountain, but to achieve for them and
in them a victory whose prolonged action (and not mere
echo) should be their eternal life. With all his power he

---

*Surely the criticism which dissolves this passage leaves us with
little but dissolving views of anything.

was there for one vast eternal deed, which can only be described as the redemption, the new creation, of the race. Nothing less could afford scope for the exercise of such power as his, if it was a power that must work to an active head, and could not be held in mere benignant self-possession, in quiescent, massive, brimming Goethean calm. The moral personality must all be put into a corresponding deed. What is the deed which gives effect to the whole tremendous moral resource of Jesus? There is not one except his death. If we reduce that simply to his life's violent and premature close, then we are without any adequate expression in action of so vast a moral personality. And it becomes but an aesthetic quantity, an object of moral and spiritual admiration, and the source of profound religious influences and impressions, but not of living faith and of eternal life. It is a grand piece of still-life, spectacular but not dramatic, with spell but not power. It can refine but not regenerate, cultivate but not recreate. And had Jesus not found in his death the regenerative outlet for the infinite moral power in his person, he would have been rent with the unrest and distraction of prisoned genius. He would have been no expression of the peace that goes with the saving power of God, peace which he then could neither have nor give.

3.   Revelation and the Bible

One finds a caracteristic theme of Forsyth's theology in this article of 1911.[1] It is not merely the Bible, but the gospel in the Bible which produces a living faith. There are three things in revelation for Forsyth. They are, first, God's pure fact and act of redeeming revelation in Christ crucified. Secondly, there is the true, but not pure, word of revelation in the apostles. Finally, there is one monument of that twofold revelation in the Bible. "If the act of salvation was bound up with a crime, need we be startled if its word is mingled with error?" The unity of that Bible must be maintained so that it might glorify the gospel. Forsyth never stated the relation of gospel to Bible more dramatically than in this essay.

> The Bible has its earthly house which must be dissolved for the sake of God's building, heavenly and eternal. It is this latter that concerns our eternity. We shall not be judged by what we thought of the Bible, but by what we did with its gospel; not by what we knew of the Bible, but by the way it made us realize we were known of God. We shall be rich not by the ore but by the gold. It is not our wonderful body that goes with us into eternity, it is our precious soul. So it

---

[1]See *Revelation, Old and New* for additional remarks and the relation of gospel to Bible.

is not the Bible, it is the gospel. We shall not read the Bible anymore when we pass from this world . . . but the gospel we shall read for ever and ever, and it will deepen upon our gaze as life unto life or death unto death.[2]

❖   ❖   ❖

From the *Hibbert Journal*
X (October, 1911)

Christian revelation is really redemption. It is not showing something, nor telling something, but doing something, and something very decisive. It is not truth about God, it is God coming as his own truth. It is truth in the form of life, God's life, God's action. And what kind of action? It is not God parting the curtains, looking out, and permitting himself to be seen in a *tableau vivant*. It is not God manifesting himself as the spiritual or the moral ideal, writing himself large to our sight, as if he were some vast and glorious constellation high in our soul's heaven. As even Jonathan Edwards said, the revealed glory of God does not consist in the exhibition of his attributes but in the diffusion of his fullness. What we need is power to be and do what we know. We know much more than we can realize. Of course we do speak of the great impressions or discoveries in man or nature as revelations, but that is using the word in a secondary sense. Revelation is really a religious word. It is not God standing in front of man, but God casting himself into the heart of man. It is God giving himself to man, pouring himself into human history, sacrificing himself for human recovery. And since sin can only see God by being saved from guilt, therefore revelation can only come home as redemption. The unholy must be redeemed into the power of seeing the holy, and the holy must so come. Therefore revelation is God as poignant as the cross, as deep as death, as active as evil, as intimate as the

---

[2]*Ibid.*, pp. 250-51.

spirit, as final and permanent as our salvation. It is God not only made flesh, nor made death, but made sin for us. It is God himself become our justification and redemption.

The gospel is the one central and final revelation which gives real and eternal value to all else we call revelation. Elsewhere we know; there alone we are known, and we know as we are known. It has not to do with science, or knowledge as knowledge, it has not to do with history as mere history. It has not to do with the mere occurrence of a fact, but with the meaning of it; and with its meaning not for the constitution of either God or man but for their will; it has to do with purpose and destiny. It does not tell us of God's metaphysical nature, but of his will and love. It does not give us a speculative theology, but an experimental. Nor does it give us a science of man. There is no revealed anthropology or psychology. Nor does it give us a history verified beyond all possibilities from a criticism merely historic. None of these is the gift in revelation. What is revealed is a teleology. It is man's destiny and God's practical guarantee of it. It is what he is going to do with us; nay, more, what he has done with us—not simply what he proposes with us, but what he has committed us to. When Christ died all died. Our divinest destiny is not simply revealed in the gospel, it is conveyed to us there. It is not written up in Christ, it is branded in; it is not written on our sky, but burnt in on our soul by the cross of Christ. It is not a matter of knowledge but of life, of action, of power, of fire, of crisis, of change; of a new world, a new humanity, rising by a new creation from the ashes of the old. We can only know it as we are changed by it. It is new light as it creates new life. At its root the Christian revelation is the Christian redemption and nothing less.

But when we say revelation is redemption we mean three things which it is not. First, it is not merely the Bible. Second, it is not merely illumination and inward light, either rational or spiritual. And third, it is not evolution; though there is evolution in it (as I shall show), and its scope develops upon us. Evolution as a complete system is fatal to it.

On this relation of revelation to evolution I do not here touch. But I should like to say a word about the second point before I go to the first.

The Word of God is not merely illumination, either rational or spiritual. Revelation is not a matter of reason apart from faith; nor is it a matter of spirit, of spiritual subjectivity, apart from the apostolic word. Mere rationalism, apart from the Christian revelation, is bound to end, where historically it has ended, in agnosticism, or in a monism which comes to much the same thing in practice. Without Christ history has no God in the end. And mere spiritualism, or trust in the inner light detached from the historic Word, destroys revelation in other ways. It swallows it up in the fogs, bogs, and flows of mere subjectivity. No religion is possible without a revelation, and no Christian revelation is permanently possible without a historic redemption. Religion without a revelation is mere subjective religiosity; and revelation which is not redemption is mere illumination, a mere branch of spiritual culture. It is its theology that distinguishes Christianity both from the world and from all other religions. Christianity is Christianity by the redemption which distinguishes it historically from mere manifestation, mentally from mere illumination, and morally from mere amelioration.

There are many today who are interested in the idea of revelation, but who are repelled by the idea of redemption. "Revelation," they say, "is not a mere theological term; it has to do with religion. But redemption is theology, and theology is mere intellectual mythology. Indeed," they say, "revelation is becoming a living idea only now. We are recovering it, loosing it and letting it go. Last century, to be sure, agnostic science immured it, locked the door, threw away the key, and wrote up 'Ignoramus et ignorabimus.' But today," they continue, "science itself turns gnostic and mystic. In the hands of the biologist, physicist, the psychicist, the historian, revelation looks out and bursts out everywhere. There are many voices, and not one of them is without signification. We must own a revelation world-wide for a world beyond. But redemption is another matter. It is an idea which belongs wholly to the past, and we escaped from it long ago." You will find Christian people, I grant, who feel or who speak like that, people at least in the churches, or not unfriendly to the church. Indeed, in many respects today the severest strain is not between the church and the world, but within the church itself. It is set up by the question whether the gospel is a religion of revelation without redemption, or whether it is a religion where revelation must be redemption. And by redemption is here meant something radical—the redemption of the conscience, redemption from guilt, forgiveness, redemption which involves a theodicy. I do not mean mere release from the poison and pressure of life; for guilt is something more than either disease or difficulty. Is redemption, is forgiveness, but one phase in Christianity, an element early and somewhat mythological, and one fittest still for the gross sinner and the less cultured circles; or is it the very essence always of any religion in which sinful man has to do with a Holy God? Is it a crude stage which we outgrow as we pass upward in spiritual refinement, and learn to see revelation everywhere as the inflow upon the soul of divine light and power? Is forgiveness and its reconciliation an interest which belongs chiefly to the first phase and lower end of the Christian life? As culture grows do we leave the notion of sin behind and demand something more psychological than theological for our spiritual food; an inner process promoted rather than an outward relation restored; a new way of construing the soul and its working, religion and its processes; an illumination in the soul instead of a reconciliation in Christ? Is it the soul coming to itself rather than to Christ—to its deep subliminal self instead of to its heavenly Savior? Is Christianity to live chiefly in that region of psychological revelation, where the deeper self has well emerged through our worldly crust and dropped all the fragments of shell; and is it then to condescend to adapt itself patiently and tolerantly to those who are in the first tumult of the eruption, in the raw redemptive stage? Is God's supreme revelation of himself some deeper depth of our nature that wells out when the subliminal fountains of our being are broken up, something that gradually emerges upon man's consciousness as he better understands the processes of the religious soul; or is it his constant and final redemption of us by a permanently super-historic act in the historic Christ?

To that question the New Testament gives but one answer from the past, and it is the condition of the church's future, as it has been the marrow of the church's long experience. By all means let our preaching of the Word grow more psychological, as skilled education does; but the Word we preach does not come by any discovered psychology of ours, it comes by God's revealed act and gift in the cross of Christ. It comes in experience but not from it, else it were no revelation. Human speech becomes the divine Word only as our words are moved, filled, and ruled by the grace of God. The gift in revelation is not truth but life, not light but power, not novelty but certainty, not progress but finality, not a new stage of evolution but a new creation, a new birth, a passage from death to life. No amount of light can annul a moral curse, no science, no intuition. And it is a moral curse on us that a saving God has to do with, as a holy God. Our hell is nothing he can slake with the dew of his pity, but something he must quench in the blood of his grace. In his love and his pity he may redeem us, as he did Israel, from outward foes; but it is in his holy grace and his holy cross that he must save us from ourselves, from our guilt, from man's fear and hate of his holy name. If that is not a situation manufactured by an old and morbid theology, it indicates the revelation we need in our last stress. It is the revelation neither of an ideal nor a lover, but of a redeemer.

I now come to my first point in connection with what revelation is not. Revelation is not merely the Bible. It is what gives value to the Bible; it is the gospel in the Bible. It is not a book saying something, but a person doing something. We may mislead the unskilled by a certain way of speaking of the Bible as the Word of God. The Word of God is the gospel, which is *in* the Bible, but it is not identical with the Bible. The soul is not the body, though it is inseparable from the body, and is the object of the body. Revelation is less than the Bible, and it is more. Its compass is very small, smaller than the Bible. So far as words go, you can pack it into a much less space. In mere statement it is simply the message of Christ living on earth, dying, risen, and living in glory, and all for God's glory in our reconciliation. You can get it into a verse like John 3:16. But if its compass is small its content is vast, infinite. It is like a soul of genius, like an eternal soul, in a small body. Its range is beyond the compass of any book. For it can only be written out on the scale of all humanity. And it is to be satisfied with nothing less than the total conquest of history, and its complete absorption in the regeneration. Christ's span of life was brief enough, yet he contains Christianity, he did not simply found it. And, moreover, above all its range in history, past or future, this revelation, this gospel, involves at its spring the whole resource of infinite God. You can have that in no possible

book or library of books, but only in the soul of Christ, in
the work of Christ, in a present Christ, in the Holy Ghost.

If revelation is, at the root of it, redemption, if it is God's
redeeming act on life, and not a mere reinterpretation of
life then it cannot be identical with a book. The book of a
great genius might interpret life anew, but it could not
redeem life. Novelty, a new problem, a fresh insight, is not
the essence of either revelation or redemption, but power
is. And yet how could this revelation reach us without a
book? Of course a book is not an act; it is the record of an
act, or it is the product, the monument, of an act. It tells
us of an act before it, or it registers the act done in producing it. The book indeed is not the act, true enough; but
yet it is quite a necessary part of the act and its effect.
What would our past be to us if we had no record of it?
What were the drama of *Macbeth* transacted in Shakespere's
imagination alone if he had not given us the play in our
hands?

Is it not clear that for a revelation like God's we must
have a book, and yet more than a book? I will put it thus.
In the strict sense, revelation has to do only with God, and
with God only in his personal relation to us. *To us.* But
then *we* are not a heap of sand. Humanity is not a mere
mass of units. It is an organism, with a history. And revelation therefore is God's treatment of us *in a history,* in a
humanity. Paul says it is to bring all mankind to the fullness
of the stature of a colossal man in Christ Jesus. If God's
treatment of us be redemption, it is a historic redemption.
Its content is the living, loving, saving God, its compass is
cosmic; its sphere is human history, actual history. The
means it must use is action, it is not literature. God does not
save man by authorship, by dropping a book from the sky,
by dictating a work of more than genius. That might be the
way of Mohammedanism, or Mormonism, but it is not the
way of the gospel. God did not save us even by inspiring

a book. He did something, which in its turn inspired the
book. Christ wrote nothing, he commanded nothing to be
written. And for both prophets and apostles, for Old Testament and New Testament, the writing was an afterthought.
The gospel gift from God is neither a book nor a genius,
but a Christ. It is himself. It is a person, an incarnation.
It is himself in history, that is to say, himself in personal,
moral action, himself acting with all his holy might in sinful
humanity and on its scale, himself made sin for us. The
gift, then, is not a book but a fact, a person, and his con-
summatory act.

But it is not even these treated as bare facts and locked
in a glass shrine like holy relics with a χάρις ἀθίκτων ἱερῶν.
They are facts with a meaning and a value. Christ's revelation is not an incident that happened to him, but an act
that he put himself into. He gave himself in it; and gave
himself, not to our historic knowledge, nor to our rational
conviction and assent, but to our living faith. And what does
that mean? Does faith mean just that we credit the fact
of Christ or of the cross? Does not everything turn on the
content and meaning of that fact, its inner value, the purpose of that act, the moral interpretation of it, the intention
and effect of it, the way God knows us in it? Especially on
this last. To know that is more than just knowing God to be
there. It is rather knowing that there we are known of
God. That is the kind of revelation that makes Christian
religion. Revelation is less being taught of God than being
known of God; and religion, faith, is knowing that we are
known, knowing *as* we are known, knowing in kind God's
knowledge of us, knowing it back again, knowing the true
inwardness of the historic fact in which we are known,
apprehending that wherein we are apprehended in Christ.

So it is not a matter of sight but of insight, of personal
response, of response with our person. The mere crucifixion
of Jesus was no revelation. Many people saw it to whom it

meant nothing more than *any* execution. It does not reach us as a religious thing, as revelation, till it receives a certain interpretation. And not any interpretation, allegorical or fanciful, will do, but the interpretation which saw God in it and especially saw what God saw in it; which saw not what he had to put up with but what he did in it, and saw that with the whole person and not with the vision alone, with an act or will and final committal and not a mere perception. Not a soul saw it in that way when Christ died. No one saw it or answered it as the act or purpose of God, only as the failure of another messiah. Therefore, besides God's act we must have God's version of his act. God must be his own interpreter. He must explain himself, and his action. We have seen that none can act for God, none reveal him, but only himself in Christ. But we must take this other step. None but himself can reveal his own revelation. "God only knows the love of God," when it comes to this. So, besides God's own act in Christ's cross, we must have, as part of it, God's own reading of it as his, and as he meant it. A man's great life-work may be to write a book revolutionizing thought, but it is useless unless he secure that it is published, read, attended to—sometimes expounded. So God's own act of redeeming is not completed without its self-interpretation. That is *his Word*. The work goes sounding on its glorious way in the Word of it, the preaching of it. The act of redeeming completes itself in the Word of reconciliation. The redeeming act in Christ goes on preaching itself in the apostles it made. Truly, God's self-revelation is done in the redeeming act of Christ—"He commendeth his own love to us in that, while we were yet sinners, Christ died for us"; but it only comes home by the Word, the *preaching*, of the apostles, whereby Christ reveals his revelation to individual experience. The apostles did not sit down to *write* as soon as they were inspired with insight into the meaning of Christ crucified. They gave

themselves up to the new Christ as they had never done
when they were but disciples, and they began preaching.
They were preaching the Word, and sending home, in his
spirit, God's act in Christ, *before* the most precious part of
the Bible was there at all—the New Testament. It was the
Word, the gospel, that made the New Testament. It was
the preached Word that completed the revelation—not the
written Word, which is but the memorandum, or the supplement, of the preaching, and reflects that kind of power.
The grand value of the New Testament, then, is that it is
the supreme monument of the apostles' preaching and action. To put it in a crescendo, it is the condensed *register*
of their spoken *insight* into God's *meaning* of his own *action*
in *Christ*. And it was the inspiration of the redeemer that
gave them this understanding. So that we might, perhaps,
put it also in this way: God smote upon the world in Christ's
act of redemption; it sounded in the apostles' word of
reconciliation; and it reverberated, and goes on doing so
in the Bible.

Have we not, then, the three things in revelation? We
have, first, God's pure fact and act of redeeming revelation
in Christ and him crucified; we have, second, his true, but
not pure, Word of revelation in the apostles; and thirdly,
we have one monument of that twofold revelation in the
Bible. (The other monument is the church, which I have not
to discuss here.)

But, "God's true, *but not pure,* word of interpretation in
the apostles"! This need make no one uneasy. Christ's interpretation, in the apostles, of his sinless self and his finished Word was done through fallible men under historic
and imperfect conditions. The sense of their translation is
sound and final, but the form is not perfect like a statue,
nor is the marble without flaws. May I remind you that
God's own act in Christ itself rose out of the very midst
of human history, and so it has pieces of that history cling-

ing to it. It did not hover over history like the cross seen
by Constantine's army. Nor was it let down on history, perfect in beauty, final in form, and four square every way, like
the heavenly Jerusalem descending out of heaven from God
merely to *alight* on earth. That is poetry, not history. The
act of God in Christ was imbedded and involved in history.
It was woven into the tissue of history. It had a long and
wide preparation in history. It was blended into the pattern
of humanity. It was grafted into the great psychology of
the race. Miraculous as it was it was that. Transcendent
as it was, it was immanent in the vast continuity of human
affairs. So much was this the case that it has created the
most tremendous difficulties for our faith. The greatest
difficulties have been created by the fact that the death
of Christ, which consummated God's purpose with the race,
was yet a judicial murder and a national crime. "Him, delivered by the determinate counsel of God, ye *wickedly*
slew." The one act in which God forgave the world was,
on its under side, an act never to be forgiven. The eternal
salvation came by what Christ called an eternal sin. I do
not go into discussion of that vast, that unspeakable problem. I only mention it to show what we must be prepared
for if we take in earnest a historic Christianity, how mixed
in its form such a revelation must be, how we must allow
discounts and rebates. I am suggesting that if that is so
with the *act* of salvation it is true also of the *Word* of that
act, and especially of the Bible *record* of that Word. Divine
truth and human error are distinguishable but inseparable.
If the pure and perfect act of God when it entered human
history was mixed with human sin in a way that baffles our
thought, need we be surprised that the Word of that act,
as *it* entered human vehicles and human story (by speech
or writing), should also be mixed with foreign and imperfect
elements in a perplexing way, and a way we cannot mark
off with scientific exactness? If the *act* of salvation was

bound up with a crime, need we be startled if its *Word*
is mingled with error? Nay, the sinless Son of God himself
—God's Word in John's sense—was, by his own consent, by
his emptying of himself, limited and wrong on certain points
where now, by his grace, we are right. I mean points like
the authorship of a Psalm, or perhaps the parousia. Need
we be surprised, then, if we find in the written Word the
limitations which were part of the incarnation of the eternal
Word? The Bible is at once a document of man's religion
and more inwardly and deeply, a form of God's Word, and
the chief form that we now have; but, as it wears a human
and historic shape, it is not immune from human weakness,
limitation, and error. The Bible is the great sacrament of
the Word, wherein the elements may perish if only the
Word itself endure. The letter of Scripture is the reverend
bread and wine, but the consecrating Word and the power
they convey is the gospel.

The Bible is there for the sake of the gospel within it.
Anything might happen to the Bible if only it glorified
the gospel. That is the true and safe perspective for us.
We must take the whole gospel for our salvation, but we
need not take, cannot take, the whole Bible. I find some
help in a way of putting it which others may think fine
drawn. I ventured once to say we need not take *the whole
Bible*, but we must take *the Bible as a whole*. Truly, we
cannot do what we are sometimes asked to do. We cannot
dissect the Word, the revelation, out of the Bible and hold
it up to be sharply seen but we can distill it. We can see
it as a finer light in light. We can feel in the Bible a fullness
which we can never put together from its parts. It is the
"fullness of the whole earth that is God's glory," not its
detail; so it is the fullness of the Bible, the Bible as a totality,
that is the Word of gospel, not a Bible in sections, texts, and
atoms. There is a Bible within the Bible emerging and en-
larging through it. That is God's saving will and work, which

he makes felt. It is the gospel of his redemptive purpose and action. The gospel, the revelation is organic in the Bible, it is not composite. It came in diverse times and manners, but as the dawn comes in different skies, and lands, and seasons; it is not pieced together as a puzzle that can be taken down. The Bible is not true in compartments. Only the lowest organisms are equally vital in each several and severed part.

And, again, this unity and fullness of the Bible, like the fullness of the whole earth, is not something to be viewed on the flat, but in a perspective. To the infant everything is equally near, and it puts out its hand for the gas as it does for its bottle. Only an experience (which we all forget) teaches us the meaning of near and far. And there is no greater difference between the trained and the untrained mind than the power of judging distance, the sense of relative values, the tact of degrees, the grasp of the hier-archy of truth; or in religion it is the measure of things according to what Paul calls the proportion of faith. To the untaught man most things, except so far as they affect his business or his bosom, are of equal and monotonous value. His world is a mere background for some form of egoism; and it is a background painted as a piece of decora-tion would be, and not as a picture—it is on the flat. It is without perspective. Heaven is as near as earth; the horizon is at the door. The man is as ready to be interested in one thing as another, if only it be made interesting. His universe is like an infinite newspaper in which items of every kind are lowered before him on one sheet of things clean and unclean. But that is not the way of life or the manner of truth. Truth and reality exist in infinite gradations; among truths there is primogeniture and prerogative; there is de-gree, priority, rank, and place; there are shades, perspec-tives, evolutions. Beginnings rise to closes; there is a de-velopment of truth as well as of time, which grows richer

and fuller always, and shows more and more the true right
to reign. The truth of the world as one universe, the truth
in which it is all destined to end, rises out of it in the
glorious hierarchy of a varied and ordered fullness, from
men, angels and archangels, to the very Son of God. Out
of a fiery mist and chaos the world rose, and out of the
world comes the wonder of human society, its ordered
discipline and achievements, the principles of genius, the
victory of the saints, and the redemption of the Son of
God; from which the church rises as the greatest product
of history, and the Bible as the senior colleague of the
church. So it is also within the Bible itself. Elements are
there which in time we leave behind, because they were
only a soil from which the ruling truths grew, a medium
from which they condensed and rose. Beliefs and cults are
shed which were but the chrysalis of living faith. The silk
is drawn off the cocoon and spun fine. Truths themselves
are refined and exalted, and lost in higher truths. Out of
the flux of imagination there crystallizes the jewel of faith.
To change the image, out of the popular religion of Israel
as a mere piece of civilization hatches the living revelation
of God, with healing in its wings. Out of tribal wars and
national deliverances rises the world's redemption. In the
midst of some Hebrew superstition emerges the prophetic
religion. Out of orgiastic dervishes develop the prophets.
Out of prophetic fantasy ascends apostolic faith. Eschato-
logical dreams ascend and come to themselves in the kingdom of heaven and the city of God. Thus as we ponder
our Bible it becomes alive not at points only, or in great
texts, but all along the swelling line. We come to see in it
a living process, in which there are continually being thrown
to the surface those things that are meant to consolidate,
and stay, and rule. And there is also a debris thrown down,
which we can then afford to leave and lose. There is a great
process of crystallization going on, and the mere bulk of

the book is no measure of the diamonds it makes. The Christian doctor, for instance, loses his belief in demons, while he gains faith in Christ who exorcised them. The preacher gains faith in the spirit as he strips off those early rhapsodies of wild seers in Israel, or the first babblings of the young church as it spoke with unruly tongues. Even Isaiah (to go back for an instance) held and spread the fatal belief that Jerusalem was impregnable; and long afterwards it created the public infatuation in which Jerusalem was overthrown; but Christ drew the heart out of the prophet's message, and founded on it a church against which the gates of hell cannot prevail. We are being taught by recent scholarship that almost every Christian belief is the sublimation and, still more, the capitalization into eternal values, of dreams or mythologies that filled the world of that time. They had worked like yeast in the generations before, and they swelled in aspiration among the peoples around. Christ said the great amen to the human prayer, but not to every petition of it. He answered its need, and not its ignorance, in asking. In the Bible the spirit of God is continually coming to itself in a creative evolution, finding itself, shedding the form of a stage to win the freedom of the goal, and keeping only the things that are before out of all the things it leaves behind. Yea, the very teaching of Christ in his apostles corrects, sublimates, and eternalizes the words of his own mouth upon earth, which were sometimes said but to the hour or the man, and did not bind the church for ever. But if ever Christ's teaching in his preaching apostles is more valuable than his teaching of his learning disciples, it is only because of his own act in the cross and in the spirit, which fulfilled and finished all. It was Christ teaching all the time, and teaching concretely, as his way was—speaking to the existing situation with the opportunism of the changeless and eternal.

Let me close by illustrating what I mean from within

the teaching of Christ himself. Take the parable of Dives
and Lazarus. Regard it for a moment as if the whole Bible
were squeezed into that tractable size. Treat it as the Bible
in small—as a bibelot. What have you there? You have the
medium and the matter, the husk and the kernel, the setting
and the jewel, the ore and the gold, the scenery and the
soul. You have the large pictorial element, the vehicle, and
within it the truth or idea. You have scenery sketched in
from the notions current at that time about the world
beyond death, and you have the truth which Christ used
these to teach. You have a background taken over ready
made from inferior artists, and you have the foreground
carefully painted by the Lord himself. The day is gone by
when we could find in the drapery of the parable a top-
ography of the future state, guaranteed accurate by the
authority of Christ. He tells us nothing of such posthumous
geography or precedure. He gives us no book of the dead.
He did not come either to correct or to sanction the popular ideas on such things. He simply made parables of them,
as in other parables he invented or remembered. He may
have shared these popular beliefs, as he knew but of a
flat earth and a revolving sun. He could treat these notions
as the mere setting for his truths. They were but fuel for his
flame.

But beyond all the scenery he had two ideas in the front
of this parable that he did mean to stamp and to wing—
possibly there may be two parables fused up in our story,
with an idea to each. First, he did want to press the truth,
which so often engaged him, of heaven *bouleversement* of
earth, God's subversion of the social verdict. He often taught
that the kingdom of heaven was in a standing irony to the
social order, that grace upset the current criteria of social
worth (as in the case of the prodigal and his brother), and
that it meant the revaluation of the moral values of the
natural order, and often their inversion—the first last and

the last first. And, secondly, he wished to send home the principle that, in spite of that grace had a moral basis, that it was not freakish, and was not magical, and was not sensational, that the soul's fate was settled by a moral revelation rather than a miraculous. "If they hear not Moses and the prophets neither will they believe if one rise from the dead." It is the moral appeal that is the marrow of the gospel, not the prodigious, not the portentous, not the thaumaturgic, not the astounding; it is the spiritual, the redemptive, not the sensational. The saving revelation is addressed to the guilty conscience, not to the domestic affections, and not to the sense of wonder. It is directed to the sinful soul and not the mind agape. Its genius is faith and not imagination, not mere sensibility; and what it would produce in us is not an impression but a confession.

Such is the gospel in this parable; it is its truth, its burden, its message. And such is the place of the gospel in the Bible. It is blended, for educational purposes, with much that has no voucher, no perpetuity. Much is scaffolding that is taken down for the house to appear. The Bible has its earthly house which must be dissolved for the sake of God's building, heavenly and eternal. It is this latter that concerns our eternity. We shall not be judged by what we thought of the Bible, but by what we did with its gospel; not by what we knew of the Bible, but by the way it made us realize we were known of God. We shall be rich not by the ore but by the gold. It is not our wonderful body that goes with us into eternity, it is our more precious soul. So it is not the Bible, it is the gospel. We shall not read the *Bible* any more when we pass from this world (so far as one may meddle with such forecasts); but the *gospel* we shall read for ever and ever; and it will deepen upon our gaze as life unto life or death unto death.

But is not all this fatal to the Bible? Is it not its destruction by modern criticism? To which may I answer that the

Christian function of death is not destruction but resurrection? The Bible would die well if the gospel lived better. In the grace and providence of God Christian criticism is doing for us what death is meant to do in the same providence. It is detaching and releasing, loosing and letting go; it is sifting the eternal gospel from the form of history and the *milieu* of time. It is distilling the precious soul from the valuable body for heavenly places—as indeed all experience is meant to do. The great function of criticism is positive. It is not negative, not fatal. Death and judgment are not there to upset all, but to set all up; they are there less to destroy wrong than to establish right. The end of judgment is righteousness. And criticism is but the Greek for judgment, and judgment is but the Latin for righteousness. So criticism is the agent of right and truth. Judgment is not a dreadful thing but a glorious, not an awful doom but a mighty hope. That, at least, is the Bible view of it. It was looked forward to. And such is the purpose and promise of the form of judgment called criticism. It is the elimination of the gospel from the religion of a certain race and from the record of a certain stage of culture. It is its clear display by a slow, careful, brilliant, and luminous search of the Scriptures. Amid all our popular neglect of the Bible in the church it has never received such attention from the *mind* of the church as it has today. The form of the attention is critical, and criticism always begins by being analytic, negative, and even censorious, because the abuse of authority leaves so much to clear away. But it ends with being positive and appreciative. It is a cleansing fire. It prunes for the sake of more fruit. And at this moment it is passing from the one stage to the other. It is passing into the positive, appreciative, and constructive stage. The Bible is not dead, it is in the course of resurrection. And in such a way as I have shown. Revelation is truly in the greatest danger from evolution; but criticism would release it from mere evolution by making the book of one age to be the preacher to all time, by distinguishing the revelation from the preacher who is only made by the revelation; and it would secure by worship of the gospel more true reverence for the Bible that grew round the gospel.

Criticism, therefore, is not to be discouraged but to be criticized. It grows to its work at compound interest, so to say, by the criticism of criticism. One school criticizes the other, correcting but continuing its tradition, and exalting its life. The higher criticizes the lower, and all is criticized by the highest, by the central revelation and gospel of grace. The Bible is to be judged by its Word, and its Word is judged by its Christ and his work—the book by the message and the message by the act in Jesus Christ.

The one fatal thing against which I would presume to protest is the vague, careless, and, forgive me if I say, lazy habit of dismissing the Bible from your interest because you have heard, because Gashmu hath said it, that criticism has knocked the bottom out of the Bible and left the sides to fall in. You do not really know that it is so, but you have vaguely heard it. The real students of the Bible do not speak in that way, the men you do not hear so much about, but who really settle things. It is only the casual, the shallow, the gossips of that region who talk so. And to judge the gospel by gossip, or the church by chit-chat, is as if you should be engrossed by the tattle of strangers about the frail and aged body in which your mother carries still a spirit so high and a faith so eternal.

4. A Rallying Ground for the Free Churches: The Reality of Grace

> We have the faith. Each church is equally earnest to do the will of Christ and represent it. What is that will? Where is it found? In history. It is not each other we have chiefly to understand, but the historic revelation which is the foundation of us all.

It is this historic revelation—the reality of grace—which Forsyth pinpoints in three dimensions as the marrow of Christianity. This concentration in church unity, simplification for church extension, and emancipation for church freedom, holds a great future for the free churches.

> A great future awaits the free churches when they rediscover their own treasure and hear again at its spring, their one call as the apostles of free and holy grace.[1]

That concentration is to the greatest fact of history, neither man's ruin nor his struggle, but to the God who on the cross appears in history as "Holy Savior of our moral wreckage unto eternal life." The simplicity must be an evangelical one—"on the simplicity of evil men converted, not of innocent little children, or of dear good men, but

---

[1]*Hibbert Journal* IV(1906), 827-28 and below.

on the simplicity of those who have tasted grace because they have tasted sin." The emancipation is simply the soul freed by the gospel to think with power about ultimate things. Therefore preachers "should study one book of Scripture thoroughly, and the whole Bible adequately."

❖   ❖   ❖

From the *Hibbert Journal*
IV (1906)

I have had much to say of late, in this journal and elsewhere, on the reality of grace as the be-all and end-all of Christianity. By the editor's favor I would say something more. To rally on this one power or doctrine as the marrow of Christianity implies three things: a great concentration, a great simplification, and a great emancipation.

It requires a great concentration in the interest of positive Christianity, of church unity; a great simplification in the interest of popular Christianity, of church extension; and a great emancipation in the interest of liberal Christianity, of church freedom.

Christianity must be positive, popular, and liberal; and the possibility of combining all three lies in the reduction of everything and the reference of everything to the authority of the gospel of grace. It is on the first head, of concentration, that I chiefly write.

I.

Concentration is in the air. For one thing, we feel the lack of it in various ways. What is the cause of the moral and spiritual uncertainty which the more positive churches try to make good by dogmatism? It is the irresolution of the public mind. It is a moral lack, the want of will, the lack of concentration, of the moral concentration involved in faith. The tap-root of uncertainty is generally irresolution somewhere. I wonder how many of the public, even of the Christian public, who have come to deny or ignore such doctrines as an atonement, ever forced themselves down to the New Testament in a thorough way. People complain that the religious ground is unsure who have never compelled themselves to examine it with a tithe of the care spent on a contract; but they have taken current suggestions in a dreamy and hypnotized way. They will not attend, they will not force themselves to attend, gravely to the gravest things. They scatter their interests with indiscriminate impartiality over the wide field of modern knowledge. They read everything in a vagrant, browsing fashion. They turn on the most serious subjects the holiday, seaside, newspaper habit of mind. They admit the subjects are momentous, but they do not treat them so. They do not own the authority of such subjects to compel special pains towards certainty about them. If a preacher fall into this frame he may coo over the people the balmy optimisms of a natural and unconscious Christianity which makes no call upon the will for positive belief, but delights those who are only at the aesthetic stage of faith and life. Is it not the case that most doubt on religious matters is listless and not vigorous, discontented rather than negative, vague and not positive? Is that not the fashion of the whole agnosticism which has replaced the old atheism? So that one is grateful to find a vigorous, serious, and informed doubter, with whom something can be done because he begins with a serious concentration on the objects of his criticism.

It is to meet this current dispersion of interest and distraction of mind that certain of the churches close their ranks, harden their face, and put down their foot with new firmness on the old paths. They concentrate upon a single and selected issue which carries all the rest. The church of Rome leaves all other doctrines for the time in the rear, and concentrates on the doctrine of the divine society, the church—with immense effect, of course, in a social age. To accept that, in the infallible pope, is to accept all doctrines with an implicit faith. Anglicanism also concentrates on the acceptance of the church, but as centered in the episcopate; or it rallies upon the principle of an establishment. Well, upon what shall those of us concentrate who cannot so think of the church? An established church is but a tolerated anachronism at this stage of history. It is a belated survival, a *succès d'estime* resting on social prestige and historic tenderness, but not on a spiritual principle. In due course it must cease. But that cohesion, that solidarity borrowed from the institutional or national principle is a great thing. Are the free churches in a condition to replace it by anything as effectual drawn from their own ethical and spiritual principle? Is disestablishment possible till they are? Federation is a great idea, but it is too shallow to be the real nexus of spiritual bodies. If they rally it must be on something in the nature of an authority—not a mere center, but a creative point sending out what Coleridge calls "organizing surges." A center is but static, an authority is dynamic. And upon what can they rally but on the source of their own call as Protestant churches in God's formative grace?*

There is great need of this renewed central control. The

---

*It should be said that throughout there is meant by grace neither God's general favor, nor his mercy to our failure, nor his pity for our pain, but his pardon and redemption in face of our sin, under such moral conditions as are implied in atonement, however construed. The Catholic sense of grace, as a *caritas infusa,* like the finest substance, is quite out of view. If the Reformation meant anything at all, it meant the submersion of sacramental grace by evangelical. I find also that it needs saying, that by the gospel is not meant a statement, doctrine, offer, promise, or boon. It is a revelation, even, only because it is a redemption. It is an objective power and historic act of God in Christ, decisive for humanity in time and in eternity, and altering for ever the whole relation of the soul to God as it may be rejected or believed.

Protestant churches, like the Liberal party, are fissiparous. At least they are not centripetal. They have a woeful lack of perspective and of the sense of values in their theology. It needs refocusing. And the only authority whereby they can concentrate with effect or adjust spiritual values is that in which they rose—that of grace and gospel. They can rally upon doctrine only as a tentative expression of God's act of gospel. They must gather, not to a point, but to a power. Observe the concentration in Christ's own case. He so bent himself on his one work of grace that he is accused of leaving whole sections of life, and even doctrine, out of his world. One thing he pursued, and it was a thing he *did;* but it was the thing which has the power and the promise of all things else. There is one thing needful for all other things, and given by none of them. But he gave it. And there is at the long last no other moral power for us but the one gospel he was straitened to accomplish. The free churches, alienated from a positive theology, have dispersed their spiritual energies over too many views and enterprises for their cohesive faith. The Free Church Federation is an attempt to counteract this by common organization and work. But federation will not do it beyond a certain point. Nor will evangelism, peripheral and peripatetic. It needs far more even than revival. It needs a rebaptism, a regeneration of the Christian mind and conscience in the churches themselves, a re-reading of their old gospel, a new type of faith and manner of theology, bringing a new penitence, a new forgiveness, a new purpose of heart and endeavor after another order of obedience. It is not evangelists we need, but apostles to re-evangelize the evangelists. A revival, not of mere piety, but of faith, of the positive power, and insight of grace, would draw together the churches of grace, the free churches, as nothing else could. And it cannot be denied that this means for the ministry a new dogma, a theological revival. For a church dogma is indispensable.

But that would come of itself. Questions of church government, even of atonement or incarnation, would settle themselves in a new, free, positive creed among churches that realized anew their religion—the power and compass of their central faith, delivered from popular triviality and debasement. A great future awaits the free churches when they rediscover their own treasure, and hear again, at its spring, their one call as the apostles of free and holy grace.

We do need to go back to our spring for our light and strength. Every age has its own spiritual problem. It interrogates the unseen with a new demand. It appeals to it with a new need. It taxes it for new power. Our age has a question and a need of its own. It is not the same as that of the Reformation. It is not exactly that of the first century. Jesus dealt with a Jewish civilization, the apostles with a pagan, and Luther with a Catholic. Luther arose amidst a Europe long exercised about questions of sin, penance, and the means of grace. His gospel to that age was the gospel of a gracious God to a sinful experience. He spoke to people who were in a church and who knew sin. But we stand in a different Europe, a modern Europe, scientific, critical, ethical, and social. We have the same gospel, rich to all, but it faces a different need. The sense of sin has died down for the time; and the ruling idea of God, if not holier, is purer than it was, richer, broader, humaner, more intimate to men and things. We speak to people who are not in a church, or who care little for the church they are in. Many of them will change their church and minister for a better tennis green on the other side of the town. The church and its message form no part of life's reality for them, but only of its decency at best. They do not deny, but ignore the Christian God. The time's demand, therefore, is not for a diviner idea of God; it is for power to realize, in experience, conduct, and thought, an idea already more divine than we can either take home or carry home in practical effect. It is not a more ideal God we need, but a more real God, actual in and over life. We know, or we dream, more things about God than we know how to use, trust, or obey. The question is not as to the ideality of Christ's character, for all own that; but it is as to the reality of his gospel, the authoritative reality, amid things, of a holy God whom our best ideas only desire, surmise, or depict. Especially it is a question as to the reality of a holy God, gracious in action, not to the church alone, but to society. With all the humane and philosophic enlargement of the idea of God during the last two or three centuries, we are still left without the certainty that it corresponds to the deep eternal reality of the stirring world. It should not be forgotten that agnosticism is the child of idealism, and not of empiricism or materialism alone. Spencer held neither. In such a world as this ideals are apt to become incredible and impracticable in proportion to their greatness; and we have to ask what is to translate the idea into experience and action; what will make an effectual power of it, make of it a religion more near and real to us than life itself is with its tremendous avidity today? It is little that a lofty idea of God will do to fortify or rule the youth who launches out into the torrent of energy and opportunity sweeping men along in a time like this, when man, nature, the world, and a career are mightier than ever before. No mere idea of God is strong enough to cope with the passionate experience of such a world—a world with such vitality in it, such capacity, such facilities, such fascination, and such fire. It needs that the divine idea become a hearty moral experience also, and a part of the man's moral reality, before it can be a guiding and saving authority in his immersion in such life. It must, however large, however imposing, become personal, searching, and real, before it can become effective, before it can cope with the personal reality of a man's imperious self. No Christian view of life, however ardent, no enthusiasm about Christ,

will do the work of personal faith which unites a man in
Christ with the central moral reality of a saving God.

And so we ask anew, from our own position—what was it
that Christ came to bring? It is feeble now to say he came
to bring a new thought of God. He brought little for the
world of thought; for the moral world, *where reality lies,* he
brought everything. He came with God himself, and not
with a picture or a guess about God; with God, not as a
finer vision, nor as a necessity of thought, but as a mightier
power, as the holy one, as the ultimate moral energy, as
the searching, judging, saving, and final reality, active in
history and life. He was not a herald, but a plenipotentiary.
God did not reveal his nature to Christ. Christ was neither
a thinker before a problem nor a poet before a dream, but
a doer before a task. God was in Christ, reconciling. Christ
had not his knowledge of God by way of revelation. His
consciousness was part of the self-consciousness of Godhead. His action was God's act. And through Christ, God
was, and now is, in history—at its real spring, in its main
stream. This Christ is the supreme contemporary of every
age and its ruling power. The spinal cord of history is redemption. The course of total history is the evolution of
grace. Christ came with God not only in evidence but in
action, in decisive, final, continuous action on the active,
historic, total soul of man. I say Christ came with God, but
I mean that God came in him, came for a world career, and
came to abide at the throne of things.

And such a gospel meets the demand of today—not for an
ideal God, but a real God. We have to secure not a new
conception of God, but a new recognition of him—a new
position for him in that sense. And that position must be in
the conscience, amid the action in which we touch reality
at last, amid the drama of things. The people that count are
the serious people who play the game instead of watching
it; and they are forced to feel that the reality of God comes

home to us only in experience, in action, in the moral region. Judgment is there; and salvation is where judgment is. The nature of reality for living men is morality. And the real power that is demanded by our actual moral condition, our sinful condition, the only God relevant to it, is the holy historic God in his act of judgment-grace—the God in the Christ we inherit, given us and not discovered, given by himself and not procured even by a Son, given to meet our moral perdition, and given in the flood of life and action's storm, in the cross which entered a nation's politics, challenged its government, sealed its dream, broke at once its delusion and its history, and in so doing secured mankind's destiny. This indispensable power is given in the cross as the spiritual fact and power in history, searching and judging to the last reality, gracious and saving to the uttermost eternity. If the world's history be the world's judgment, the cross of Christ is the *nodus* of that judgment. The point may be clear. Reality is in morality; and morality lies in action, in history; and the need and the core of moral history, as we actually find things, is redemption—the gracious, pardoning, delivering God.

The new problem draws new depths and new resources out of the old answer. We want a God real, not only to our thought, our piety, our devotion, but to our life's action, private and social, industrial and national. Our first want is not a real religion but a real God as the practical moral power in life and society, whom to know is the solution of life and the consummation of the race. We do possess sincerity in our faith; it is reality we need—the absolute certainty that we are, amidst time, on the rock eternal, and the joyful power to place the holy God in eternal control of our experience and conduct. This is something we do not necessarily acquire by being satisfied with the historic evidence for every fact recorded in the New Testament. And when we do attain it, we feel that our experience is a function of the gospel act in Christ, an energy of Christ living in us. We need, perhaps, more preachers who feel that their great contribution to Christian reality lies not in outward and public energies, but in the strenuous silence which goes less to make scholars than to master the gospel word on the problems of personal and social life. The Reformers preached God as the gracious forgiver of a world concerned about its sin. Well, we must preach the same grace of the cross to a world less concerned about sin and more about society, a world casting about for a moral authority for the soul and the public. Each need is met by the same gospel and authority of redeeming grace. In the cross grace to sin is one with judgment to wrong. In the atonement the mercy that heals the heart is one with the final judgment that goes to the last reality of actual life. The last judgment took place in principle on the cross. And perhaps it is the element of judgment contained in grace that the present hour needs most. It is Christ's insatiable, unsparing moral reality that this age needs to have preached to it more than his comfortable words. The note is as urgent in his death which we evade as in his teaching which we receive. And perhaps the form of message which the hour will hear is Christ's first word to men rather than his last—when he began by preaching the kingdom so severely gracious, and before he found that his great work for it was in the relation of its grace to sin. But the same word of exigent, generous holiness pervaded all—holiness, the supreme form of moral personality and action. The redeemer is the mediator (and the only mediator) to us of a living, judging God, who works and weaves in all history, and saves it to eternal life through a world-tissue of moral crises centering in the cross. Christ, in his historic and public work of judgment-grace, is the one ground of soul-certainty to us; for we have to do with a problem which is historic and social above all else, and which centers on the public issues of good and evil, sanctity and sin. It is a work reported by documents as a past actuality, but it is not therefore evidenced as present reality. The reality of life lies not in reason, but in action, experience, morality. It is ethical rather than rational. The last cognizable reality emerges in the moral world of our sin and our redemption, the world whose center is the saving act of a God above all things holy—moral even to holiness. Is there a moral power in history? Is this identical with the last reality? Only the atoning redemption secures us in that faith. For the cross is that power *in nuce*. There God appears in history as holy Savior of our moral wreckage unto eternal life. The greatest fact of history is neither man's ruin nor his struggle, neither the human tragedy nor the human epic, but the gospel, the divine, composite, and continuous fact of God, sin, redemption, and eternal life—a holy God, a solidary, ruined race, a grace atoning, forgiving, redeeming, reconciling all, and an everlasting kingdom.

We must concentrate on God's act of grace rather than on Scripture as such. It is no longer enough to show that a certain position is biblical, *i.e.* is found in the Bible. There are positions taken by biblewriters which are not compatible with each other or with the gospel. There are survivals, even in inspired men, of traditional and popular views which it was the business of revelation to correct and supersede. We must show that the position is not only biblical but Christian, that it is in inner necessary connection with the grace in Christ. But even when that is done, all is not done. The revelation must be found to be not only Christian but true. The grace must be shown to correspond with the ultimate reality of human life at its most tragic and exigent. It must be in a form equal to coping with the most flushed and demonic power of mind and will. Christ himself is Christ for us, he is the very Son of God, because in his work of grace he is, by power of holy, loving will, moral master of the most titanic, Napoleonic wills in history, master of

the superman, and one therefore with the last reality of the
world. How is this to be shown? Must it be exhibited for
every Christian? Certainly not for every Christian in a scientific and theological way. The humblest Christian's faith
indeed rests on the final foundation of the world. It sets
him on the rock of ages. What saved him was the world-
salvation. But he may have little sense of the depth on which
he rests. Yet in the message of the whole church to the
great world we must show that Christ in his saving act is
identical with man's last reality of moral experience; that
the judgment in the cross is really the last, the ultimate
judgment of God on human things, and that the grace there
is our eternal destiny. And this must be set forth by the
church with a view to the world, and not the individual
merely—that is to say, theologically, and not religiously only.

The experience of the humble Christian cannot be transferred to become the conviction of another. Experience
ought to be supplemented by demonstration of a more objective kind—our personal witness should be reinforced by
some demonstration of the spirit and of power. This may
be the collective experience of the church. Or it may be the
authority of our first historic revelation in the person of
Christ, with its unique effect on our last moral extremity.
But there must be some means of making good the truth of
our Christian faith beyond the limits of personal experience
and its mere testimony. We must be in a position to go
beyond "this he has done for me," and declare "this he must
be for you." Otherwise we should be condemned, as so
many disastrously are today, to a subjective individualism
and its public inefficiency. We should be telling our experience with humility instead of preaching a gospel with authority. Peter's experience is to Paul but external testimony
which does not carry divine authority. The church is in
trust of more than its own experience. It has an objective
gospel which called it into existence, and which found and

changed both Peter and Paul; and a Holy Spirit which is not simply the sum of its experiences. The church's work can only be done as its origin came about—by a gospel of grace to the conscience through a historic person and act objective to the conscience, yet welcomed and naturalized in the conscience as morally akin to conscience, nay, as being its eternal self.

This is a theological gospel no doubt. And it must be heartily cultivated both by the pulpit and the pew. The pew must participate. And therefore such a gospel must not rest on the data of science, either physical or metaphysical. It must be based neither on the axioms of nature research nor in the recesses of reflection alone, but upon those moral foundations that underlie the practical world and the general conscience. The truth of Christianity must rest on a view of life which starts with the primacy and finality of the moral, recognizes the wreck of the moral, and presents the grand problem as the restitution of the moral. Christianity stands or falls as the religion of moral realism, and therefore (having regard to our actual state) of holy redemption. Let us not talk so much at this juncture of the divine beauty of Christ's character. Assure us of the divine reality of his gospel. I am tired of beauty, and desperate about my own doing and undoing. "We tire of all things," says Comte, "of acting and of thinking, only not of loving." Seize me with what God's love and grace have done for me and my sin to the foundations of the moral world and the far reaches of holy eternity. It is in the conscience that we touch bottom and begin to rise. Neither Christian faith nor theology can do anything with the man who deliberately denies moral obligations and a moral universe. But, denied or admitted, these moral relations are every man's affair. In the moral world alone do we find every soul's final self. And Christianity is real as it appeals to that world, and gives it supreme effect. Christianity is more real than other religions, as it more deeply appeals to that world and its actual case. And especially as it takes note of the world's moral bankruptcy and derangement by sin; and as it effectively re-establishes upon the wreck the holiness of the moral idea—the holiness of God in Christ. The power that does that is the supreme authority and reality of the world.

> There, where one center reconciles all things,
> The world's profound heart beats.

That is what is done in the redeeming work and gospel of Christ. And the grace in Christ is the supreme authority to replace at last every power that has risen up, even in Christ's name, in its stead.

But how poor is the ethical training, the discipline in moral realities, supplied to those who are to be the leaders and representatives of the church! How irrelevant to life's moral reality is much of their training! How flat, how physiological, how unimaginative is much of the psychology! How devoid of human interest much of their theology! How little it is a part of their religion, how lightly dispensed with! How hard to get even them to think in moral categories, and take impregnable stand in moral finality! How often they are troubled by metaphysical, or even biological, considerations, in which they should only be interested. Among the studies preparatory to theology there is none one misses so much (apart from acquaintance with the New Testament) as a course in moral philosophy. Moral culture is not taken seriously, compared with intellectual or religious. Men do not learn to handle moral quantities. They are unfamiliar with the calculus differential to ethical ideas. They have no real schooling in moral thoughtfulness, moral categories, moral methods and processes, the moral imagination. Something is lacking, therefore, in their grasp of the gospel, not only as a moral power, but as the focus of human conscience and the locus of human reality. And so they rush out to seek reality amid all kinds of energies and enterprises, which keep them busy and successful—and send leanness into their souls. Their ethic may be very genuine, but it only adheres to the gospel, without being evolved from it. In some it replaces the gospel.

I should welcome in the curriculum of our theological colleges less attention to the details of textual criticisms, and more given to the ideas of whole books, and the waxing import of the whole Bible. And I write with the sympathy of some whose duty lies in these detailed departments. It is quite necessary that students should learn by select passages the scientific methods of dealing with the text of Scripture. But it is more needful still that they should gain a greater familiarity than they seem to have with the whole field of biblical ideas on the one hand, and with moral theology on the other. Too much of our theology is speculation instead of evangelical thought. It is thinking out *a* gospel instead of *the* gospel, or it is pious fantasy, fruit tinned or sweetened, instead of fresh from the tree of life. Men should learn these ideas and ethics as living things, as the fundamental powers not only of the church, but of the historic soul of social man. They should learn them as becomes the students of the great preaching record which the Bible is. They should learn to find God's sermon, the Bible, more attractive and fertile in ideas than the volumes of sermons on which some preachers spend too much of their time at the cost of their originality.

> Only know
> That when half-gods go
> The Gods arrive.

To be real, we must keep in touch with the last reality. To be original, we must keep in vital contact with originals. To build well, we should quarry much in the pit from which we were digged. Men should be taught in college how to do this for themselves when they are left to themselves. They should, with all their getting, get purviews of the widest, deepest Bible world, especially in relation to the chief problems of current culture and of actual life. They should study one book of Scripture thoroughly, and the whole Bible adequately. They should be discouraged from accumulating all kinds of extraneous degrees, and be made to concentrate on the degree that belongs to their work. A variety of academic distinctions in science, say, may still leave them juvenile in their religious mind, with the tactlessness of the commonplace, and a total lack of moral imagination. Half the time bestowed on Shakespere would have served them much better. No man is competent to be a teacher of the New Testament, or to handle for the people, as a minister should, the greatest matters of faith and mind, on the basis of an ordinary degree without theological training. I do not care what cases you quote. It is unjust to the gospel to send out men to pick up theology out of casual reading and personal religion; for a young man may issue from college loaded with honors and with no gospel at all—nothing beyond raw Christian piety. He has then to experiment with a church in acquiring convictions which should have been his message. He is apt to announce as discoveries things long left as debris in the route of discovery, and to parade as new what due knowledge of the past would have shown to be not only old but superannuated. It is not respectful to the churches. It slackens their tone and their testimony. And in no other profession would it be tolerated. It would not be in business. I write, of course, of the settled pastor, not of his helper, the evangelist. Let the student, by all means, be taught in his philosophic work the great place science or literature occupies in the world of thought, but only so that the whole world of thought and tragedy find its proper place in the moral world, and that again in the realm of the gospel.

II.

Besides moral concentration, we need also much simplification and popularizing of faith. For popularity there must be simplification. The preacher must press a creed that every Christian can verify by his own experiences; and this creed is the faith in saving grace. The demand for simplicity is just, but it has gone astray in many feeble directions which only dilute the gospel in the effort to popularize it. The common idea of a simple Christianity reduces it to a natural Christianity refined and spiritualized. The elementary human emotions or sentiments are simply directed on Christ. Christ is admitted to the highest place in the circle of tender and family affections. But the simplicity which is in Christ is one thing; the simplicity in which Christ is, is another. The simplicity in Christ was for Paul sincerity of soul rather than simplicity of creed or affection. It was sincerity of soul towards a supernatural and saving Christ, rather than simplicity of belief about a natural and admirable Christ. It was a single-minded, whole-hearted personal trust in his redeeming grace. It was simple, as opposed to ritual, casuistry, and dialectic; it was not simple in the sense of being easy and natural to man. The gospel is free, but not easy. To make life easier is not the object of the gospel, only of the modern church. Grace is simple because inexplicable—as conscience is simple with its severe, inexplicable imperative. The natural man is lazy to spiritual things. For him simple means only effortless and instinctive. Love is natural and easy, so he reduces to love the supernatural and costly grace of God. Too many are offering the public a religion without moral tax—the poetry of suffering, the beauty of sacrifice, the charm of holiness, without the positivity, the cruciality of the cross. But faith is not an instinct or a taste. The gospel does not appeal to the instincts, in spite of the modern pulpit. Christianity is not an instinct. The instinctive man is enmity against God, against the gospel God with his rebuke, and demand, and absolute claim. To one who comes from a simple instinctive life Christianity is an act of hard faith. It is hard to think shame of oneself. It is hard to believe in the kingdom of God as the sure issue of history with recent Russia before our eyes, or war, pestilence, famine, earthquakes, and volcanoes. And when we master these things, it is hard to live the life of the faith we have won. But yet how simple in its severity and in its goodness the gospel is! How entire the sincerity of Christ, how profound his reality! How hard for human nature to realize! Upon such evangelical simplicity the permanent popularity of the gospel must rest—on the simplicity of evil men converted, not of innocent little children, or of dear good men, but on the simplicity of those who have tasted grace because they have tasted sin. All the curse of the world is in sin, and all blessing is in the sinner's gospel.

Religious experience is very well, and knowledge of the human heart and its literature and art is very well; but Christian faith is faith neither in our experience nor in our energies; and it is not preoccupation with them, but rather faith in something external and given, faith not in experience but in something experienced, faith which lives in definite Christian categories prescribed by the nature of God's historic gift, and not by our native sympathies. And if we become detached in practice from that something given us in the Bible alone, all our Christian experience and church life will only leave us in coteries of decadent and false sentiment. We may try to become more natural and human in our religious vocabulary, but in the process we may be making a present of the new nature to the old, and making Christianity but a refined humanity, with tasteful or tender affections. And far better for us is the broad, blunt, forceful, popular voice than the voice of an ethereal coterie. Nothing demoralizes our word more than the spirit of the coterie. We lose not only Bagehot's "note of animal passion," but the note of moral reality and the seal of spiritual power. And no grace of manner, no ubiquitous energy, no aesthetic philter can take the place of that. Not all the growth of humane and sympathetic piety can give us the moral control which flows from the gospel alone. Christianity has indeed a native tendency on one side of it towards this Catholic tone of culture and charm, delicacy and finish, like a cathedral service. And here it has been the greatest of all contributors to the diffusion of a fine civilization. But culture is not Christianity. The former is often but the elder brother in the parable. (I have been surprised at the number of cultivated Christian people who have frankly said that their sympathies were all with the elder brother, and not with the prodigal, where Christ's certainly were.) Why has not the moral progress of Europe kept pace with its culture, whether of science, taste, or manners? Why is ethic so far behind civilization? I recall the saying of a great Christian thinker who declares that in the matter of social morality there has been no progress at all by comparison. To be sure we do not walk our prisoners of war through the streets of the capital in the wake of the conqueror. We do not torture our criminals, and we do not beat our wives. And many more horrible things we no longer do. But progress in civilization is not progress in virtue. We have only to think of the atmosphere of the old Italian republics, brilliant, elegant, cruel, and vicious to the last degree. We have but to remember how, when Rome mastered Greece, she was impressed with the rascality of Greek commerce as much as with the charm of Greek culture. I could quote, if need were, the weighty opinion of Ranke to the like effect. Progress in humanity is not necessarily progress in morality. It is progress in individual sentiment or taste more than in public ethic—as we may note in the public discussions of any great social question among ourselves today. It may be kindness more than rectitude, and charity more than justice; just as the cross comes to be loving sacrifice more than holy atonement. And why, one may ask, has there been this disheartening disparity between the one development and the other? There are, of course, some reasons in human nature. Aesthetic culture is delightful, moral culture is painful. One tends to self-expression, the other to self-discipline. A good conscience, too, cannot be bequeathed like property or culture. But the great reason is that the whole church in Europe has been more or less tongue-tied with its gospel.

Institutions, which are so valuable for ethics, may also kill ethics. And in this case they have, at least, maimed them. Theologies, churches, biblicisms, and pietisms, much as they may have helped, have here arrested or deflected the moral power of Christianity. In a word, Catholicism has lamed the native moral power of the gospel. By Catholicism is meant here love detached from evangelical grace, order from personal sanctity, progress from inspiration. It called out the saving protest of the Reformation at one decisive point, and it must continue to call it out for the sake of society. More is meant, of course, by Catholicism than simply the Roman church. I mean the supremacy of the institutional or the humane element, the "Pelagian, Franciscan, Erastian" element (as Harnack calls it), in any form of Christianity. I include the Catholic survivals in some Protestant orthodoxies and in many Protestant humanisms. The humane subjectivism of the present hour threatens us now as the scientific subjectivism of the orthodoxies did once.

How very many cultivated Christian people have no idea where they are in belief! And how many of these, again, do not know how ignorant of their ignorance they are! We are often invited to let learning alone, and produce more practical ministers and clergy. Have those who talk so any idea of the extent to which practical activity covers intrinsic bewilderment among Christian people? This active nescience is a frame of mind that must tell upon our churches both in pulpit and pew, that reduces both to a sympathetic brotherhood of uncertainty and incapacity before the problem of the world; that robs the gospel of authority, the pulpit of moral dignity, and the people of the guidance to which they are entitled; that lowers insensibly the tone of our communities, and allows the meaner interests to raise their head; that deprives the church's word to the world of weight and power, and that casts the public for guidance upon the publicists and litterateurs. It moves the center of gravity from the mind and conscience to the energies and sentiments. And, however harmless that transfer might be in some cases, in the case of a religion which is nothing if not the regeneration of the conscience it is a very ominous thing. I must sometimes, I fear, have seemed to speak without due respect of the sympathetic element in our faith and work. Far be this from me. But, in the first place, those can often do most with sympathy for others who have learnt to do without it for themselves. And, in the second and weightier place, I have nothing even to hint against this precious thing except when it is made the essence of Christianity and the substitute of schooled faith with moral intelligence. To set over a Christian community a man who has but felt and never measured the gospel, whose only qualifications are raw zeal, ready piety, and fluent sympathies— however sincere he may be, is this not treason to the gospel, injustice to the church, and cruelty to souls in the end? Is it not sending nurses when we need doctors, and comforters when we need apostles and critics? We were saved not by broad sympathy, but by deep and judging sanctity. And the sin we are saved from is not a malady which calls for kindly healing, but a revolt which needs to be reduced by moral conflict, labor, and sorrow on some one's part. Our sin is not simply alienation of sympathy, but rebellion against duty and loyalty to a Father's authority. If faith stagger, and lose its vision or strength in a haze of piety, no development of our human sympathies will do more than mitigate an evil it cannot cure.

> Fools to brood and dream of easement
> When a cure alone could ease.

Sympathy may even be acute enough to see and deplore the real lack which it is not strong or profound enough to supply. Sympathy even with Christ—I will go farther, and say the very love of Christ—might be so cultivated as to cast entirely into the shade of faith in the redeemer and his redemption. So that the whole economy of atoning grace, while not denied, is only kept as in some houses you find the old spinning wheel kept in the warm drawing room.

III.

A brief word as to the emancipation we need. We want no reactionary movement, but light and air. What a release from the Pharisaic tradition and its detail was brought by Paul! What a liberty came with the gift of the Holy Ghost! What a relief Luther offered the world from the farrago of the church! And how freely we can sit to much exacting but outlying belief when we are secured in the central grace of the gospel! It is not indifference, we all know, that is the mother of toleration, but conviction. And it is only the certainty of faith in grace that can give us freedom of thought about God. The believing mind is the clear mind. Devotion brings with it a wondrous lucidity and largeness. It is only a secure faith that can give a free account of itself in theology, and leave the like freedom to others. It is only the soul freed by the gospel that is free to think with power about ultimate things. The church must be liberal as well as positive—nay, liberal because positive. What makes it positive makes it liberal, and nothing else can. Liberty is the native manner of a grace whose nature is to redeem.

And to concentrate on the article of grace alone would enlarge the church also to the freedom of a true comprehension. No other principle of comprehension will make more than a mélange; but this is an organizing principle both positive and flexible. What penetrates most co-ordinates most. All doctrines in a church are free which are compatible with free grace, and not merely found in the same book. A closed system that prescribes all belief is a great load. The burden of an elaborate corpus of doctrine is greater than the gain from its positiveness of definition. Even the Roman church could not carry Thomas's *Summa* if it were dogmatized in a body, and declared as of obligation for faith. But a center that creates life gives liberty with it. And the grace that created doctrine can continually re-create it. Some liberal churches have been seeking rational freedom at the cost of evangelical. They have pursued freedom of thought and not of soul. But rational freedom is a narrow field after all. Thought cannot be free, and should not. It is limited by fact and reality. We are only free as our master-reality makes us free. And that reality is the person of God in action in Christ. Our limit is but our fuller life. The soul alone can be free, and free only as released by grace into communion with the infinite person and saving purpose of its God.

5.   The Church's One
Foundation

This 1906 essay reflects Forsyth's positive evaluation of
the Reformation. The Reformation note of faith in free,
redeeming grace resounds in every paragraph. Through his
study of Ritschl and reading of Melanchthon, Forsyth saw
that the moral nature of faith, or the "benefits of Christ" are
much the crux of Christian belief. There is one note common
to those who find the ground of faith in the personal word
and work of the historic Jesus (Ritschl and Schleiermacher)
and those to whom the object of faith is the whole New
Testament Christ, the whole biblical Christ (Kähler). That
note is "the supreme Reformation note of the free, unbought, saving grace of God to our sin . . . . That is Christianity." [1] To further emphasize identity of the church's one
foundation with this Reformation note, Forsyth uses the
Reformation phrase, *iustificatio injusti*. This antithesis of
gospel and law leads Forsyth to conclude:

> The Reformers, like Melanchthon, said it was only
> when we realized this that we began to be intelligent
> Christians. The one central doctrine of grace has in it
> the promise and the potency of all the truth, love, joy

---

[1] *London Quarterly Review* CVI(1906), p. 196 and below.

and sanctity that the future can demand from the Bible and the church.[2]

* * *

From the *London Quarterly Review*
CVI (October, 1906)

There are three views concerning the science and the object of our Christian faith which mark the present state of opinion on this vital theme.

First we have the group of men, scholars and philosophers rather than theologians, who detach the historic Jesus entirely from the living Christ, so far as continuity of person and action goes. The extreme spirits among them treat the idea of a living Christ as an *exitiosa superstitio,* when they use plain language. The matter of their Christianity is but a Christian principle or an ideal Christ, to which the historic Jesus contributed but as a supreme seer might. And such ideas as his own pre-existence, grace, resurrection, redemption, and even sin are not contained in the teaching of this seer, nor suggested by his life; but he has been submerged by them. They were imported into the church even within New Testament times, by men like Paul, who were deeply imbued with notions current in Judaism and drawn originally from Babylonian and Egyptian speculation. Just as half a century ago we were asked to account for New Testament theology by hellenic influences from the West, so now we are bidden explain it by semitic influences of a gnostic character from oriental peoples outside of the ethical monotheism of Israel. Paulinism thus becomes a mere syncretism foisted on the historic Jesus. Christ, it is said, was not a Christian if the Pauline system be Christianity. Paul began the fatal error of Christian history—the error of identifying the Christian principle with the person of Christ.

We should welcome any light upon the historic origin of ideas which suffused the spiritual world into which Christ came, and which offered a calculus for handling the

---

[2]*Ibid.,* p. 202.

reality that entered our experience in his fullness. But all oriental doctrines of redemption were but speculative till God's act of real life came in the cross. The great Pauline ideas, in so far as they existed before Christ, and outside his circle, were not heaped mythically upon the prophet of Nazareth, but were seized by the unutterable experience of him, and used as a providential language, however inadequate, to convey some notion of what he had done and become for his own. They were the prolegomena of revelation; and themselves in their degree revealed. But the core of Paul's theology was by his own account delivered to him from the other disciples. And we have no more right to isolate the death and resurrection of Jesus from his subsequent life, and his life now, than from his earthly life preceding.

A second group would include those who do find the ground of our Christian faith in the personal word, life, suffering, and work of the historic Jesus. The historic Christ is the inner life of Jesus expressed in these things, and printing itself as the full and final revelation of the Father upon the heart and conscience of those who first came under his influence thirsting for a divine kingdom and eternal life.

To this school (if school we may call it) the death of Christ is the sealing of his life's revelation and effect rather than anything more. And his resurrection and continued life form more of a corollary than a vital element—in the faith of the individual at least. The essential thing here is not, as in the previous group, humanity's ideal Christ planted on Jesus, but God's historic revelation of his grace in him. On the other hand, the sole action of this Christ is upon man, and not upon God. It is historic action; and it continues to be historic, even if caused by the living Christ today. It is action on man and on his evolution; and the work of Christ has no bearing on God. Our justification is our progressive sanctification. The necessity for his death lay only in the actual subjective condition to which man had come. It was a sacrifice to the hardness of our hearts. It was to soften them. The 'must' lay not in any demand arising out of the holy nature of God and its satisfaction, but in the ignorance or self-will of man. At bottom Christ was not the one redeemer but the supreme impressionist.

This position is associated more or less with the name of Ritschl, following on Schleiermacher. And it is not to be denied that it has its place or right in an evangelical church, even if we think it is incomplete, and inadequate to the real moral situation of man. Its headquarters are in the Gospels rather than the epistles. But its center of gravity is still Hebraic, not gnostic, and its line of descent runs through the Old Testament. It is not oriental in any other and more pagan sense.

The third group consists of those who urge that the object of our faith is not primarily the Christ of the Gospels but the whole New Testament Christ, the whole biblical Christ, taken as a unity, without, of course, insistence on historic or speculative details. The total effect of Jesus, they say, was something larger and deeper than the second group allows. It was something whose essential genius is expanded in the theology of the epistles, and continued in the evangelical and catholic tradition of the church. When Christ rose in the soul of the apostles, and especially Paul, it meant as much for history (though not for eternity) as when he rose from his grave. The faith of the first disciples and of all the truest believers has been a faith in Christ as the objective conqueror of sin, guilt, death, and woe, and a propitiation in some sense to God (though made by God) and not to man alone. Much turns in this view on the essential and supreme place of the risen, the living, reigning, and governing Christ, and upon the effective and permanent relation of his death not only to the demands of man's sin but still more to those of God's holiness. It is urged that the death of Christ was more than a supreme testimony enacted by God to man, and that in some sense God's judgment of sin fell on him and he took the chastisement of our peace.

Now there is one note which is common to the last two groups I have named, and which is to both equally vital. And that is the supreme Reformation note of the free, unbought, saving *grace* of God to our sin, a revelation made in Christ's redemption once for all, to an experimental faith on our part which is faith in that grace and nothing else. That is the gospel. That is Christianity.

A dream which has much engaged some minds is the surmise of what it might be for Christianity if all sections of Christians should ever be persuaded in deed and truth to make this matter of grace the one article of the church by which it stands or falls. It is simply the Reformation doctrine of justification by faith, only stated objectively instead of subjectively, as the time requires. There was no undue subjectivity about that doctrine in the faith of the Reformation age, partly owing to the view of Scripture then current. But since that time a great change in the direction of subjectivity has passed over the Reformation church. And an objective of a firm but simple kind has become an urgent need.

Faith has come to dwell on itself as a pietism; or else it has glided into a humanist love which calls only for a reciprocal love on the divine side, or vice versa. But while the counterpart of love is love, the counterpart of faith is grace. And if we are to surmount a mere genial theism it is necessary that our faith be stated, not in terms of itself and the love it works to, but of its source and object—the God who in Christ is not merely loving to the lovable, but gracious to the malignant. Such a brief but pregnant statement would, of course, only be the potent minimum for the church's comprehension; it would not express the maximum of the church's thought. But it would be a whole theology *in nuce,* and theology neither as academic nor speculative, but as practical, experimental religion. It would have the power, and it would give the freedom, to produce a very varied theology or theologies. Indeed, it would make theologies a necessity. But it would be of the *esse* of the church, while these were only of its *bene esse*. And the greatest scope would be given to all varieties of theoretical belief which were not plainly or professedly incompatible with the fundamental theme. I do not raise the question whether this central theme should take formal shape, with subscription, as is the tradition of some churches, or remain a tacit and honorable understanding, as with others. Much would be gained if it were understood that the church and its theology rests wholly and creatively on this eternal and living act of God's grace to sin, and that the renunciation of this alone puts people outside the pale of gospel ministry.

By grace, it should be said, is here meant on the one hand nothing vague and on the other nothing rigid: nothing merely sympathetic, as with the anti-dogmatists, and nothing subliminal, as with the Catholics. That is to say, it does not mean, taken loosely, the kindness of the Father to his children, nor, taken literally, a hierurgic charisma, a *qualitas infusa,* or state of the soul-substance more or less below consciousness. It is not condescension to human weakness, nor is it a favor shown to human worship. It is a matter of personal relation. But it is a relation of reconciliation and not mere complacency. It is the forgiving, redeeming act of holy love to human sin, an act ultimate and inexplicable. It is not mercy to our failure, or pity for our pain, but it is pardon for our sin. The vaguer uses of the word are certainly found in the Bible, and especially in the Old Testament. Even with St. John the word means graciousness, and the more specific sense is with him gathered under the word love. It was St. Paul that went to the heart of the matter, seized the real mind of Christ, the core of revelation, and preached God's free and holy act of reconciliation by forgiveness as the central differentia of Christianity. And he appropriated to this use the word grace. It therefore designates that which makes Christianity divine and final, that which is the essence of Christ's person and work. It is grace in this sense that was the one motive of the Reformation. The call and genius of that movement was to recover the idea of grace from its Catholic deflection through pagan ethic and mystical metaphysic. It was to make the idea of grace once more religious, historic, and experiential, after being philosophized and theologized for more than a thousand years. Apart from that issue the Reformation would have been a mistake. If that issue be sent to the rear we may as well prepare for the re-catholicizing of every Protestant land in due slow course. If love be preached, meaning thereby the apotheosis of human affection, and not what Paul meant distinctively by grace, then there is no such call for Protestantism as would justify its schism within the church. A Roman church reformed upon the lines of Erasmus would have been a better agent of the mere love of God than either the Lutheran or the Reformed, and far better than the humanist or rationalist church, so popular for the hour. If the theologians are to be ruled out, let us take our Christianity from Christian scholars rather than from the litterateurs.

One ought not perhaps to speak as I have done of the *mere* love in God. I mean nothing irreverent, for in so speaking I refer really to something which is not in him— a love which is not holy and is not made perfect in grace, a love which is gracious by the way instead of culminating in grace, which exercises forgiveness as but an incident in his relations with man instead of as a redemption, re-creation, reconstitution of the race. *The* gift in grace is not mere kindness, and it is not directly moral reformation, but it is religious pardon as a new life with all moral amendment latent in it. It is religious redemption under moral conditions (secured in the propitiation). What comes to us primarily is not a *qualitas infusa,* an *altior virtus,* a miraculous *habitus* of the man, but a personal reconciliation with God. It is rather an attitude, or disposition, or experience, than an actual state. It is not charismatic but pneumatic, not a gift to life but the gift of life. It is entirely bound up with the person and work of Christ as the power of God unto salvation. Faith is the soul's answer to his grace, it is not the heart's answer to love. It is nothing else than personal trust in the personal God in Christ, the personal response to, and appropriation of, God's own personal and eternal act of pardoning and redeeming grace in Christ. It has intellectual implicates, of course, as a poem implies truths which do not rise to the surface and take explicit shape. Only the assent does not precede the trust, but is included or 'suspended' in it. Knowledge, assent, and trust are not three separate acts, but three factors in the one act of faith—just as faith, hope, and love, these three, 'abideth' as the singular totality of the Christian life—with the love ever working to the top, but possible only as the fruitage of the rest. And the only vehicle of grace is neither a sacrament nor is it human nature at its best in Jesus, but it is the Word of God—first as Christ, then as the Holy Spirit in Bible and in church. Grace is no attribute of God, but the content and action of God's will; yet it is not a will of general beneficence for our well being, but of universal mercy for our salvation, a will not merely to bless the dear but to redeem the lost. The Christian idea of God in his one revelation in Christ is not a benignant God who redeems, but a redeeming God who blesses. By God's grace, then, is meant that distinctive and central element in Christianity which I am at some pains to define. One would deprecate anything like a hypostasis of a divine attribute in speaking of the grace of God. Grace, so far from being one of God's attributes, is the very being and person of God in a certain action on us. The word has no other

sense than is implied in the more accurate phrase, a gracious
God. When this gracious God became incarnate in Christ
he did not send either an agent, a function, or a factor. He
came. The whole Godhead was there in the sense of being
involved in our redemption.*

We are all impressed by the evils of our divisions. It is
the principle of unity that we lack and look for. We do not
concentrate. We waste the attention, the seriousness, the
passion, that should move us there on secondary issues,
which by themselves distract and enfeeble us. We try to
draw from low and outlying sources power which can only
flow from the upper springs. We shall never really attain
the unity of the church, or its effect on the world, till we

---

*Is it not very striking that the deadly foes of Christ were men
who believed passionately in creed, conduct, and charity? His slayers
were people who believed to the death in God and in forgiveness, in
alms to the poor, and in sympathy to the sorrowful. God was their
passion, righteousness their watchword, redemption their grand hope,
and benevolence nothing less than a sacrament. Such was pharisaism.
So much it had in common with Christ. The deadly conflict was not
about monotheism, pardon, nor philanthropy. But it was about a matter which has sunk with us to a mere theologoumenon outside 'simple
Bible teaching'; it was about the terms of forgiveness. There lies the
essence of Christianity. The pharisee said salvation was a *justificatio
justi,* his vindication. The righteous were forgiven their shortcomings
out of regard to the matters on which they did not come short. Just as
we say that the good side of human nature will at last submerge and
justify the rest. But Christ said it was a *justificatio injusti,* a forgiveness
unaffected by the good in the sinner, and wholly due to the free
grace of God, a grace as free, unbought, undeserved, and inexplicable
as the original choice of Israel. For Christ no less than for Paul the
whole Christian issue turned on this grace of God to wickedness, not
on mere mercy to failure; and it was not for a loving God merely,
but for a gracious God he died. If we let that go, no gospel of love
alone will save us from pharisaism, which will come by the way of
Catholicism and its semi-pelagian humanism. And to let it go theologically is nothing to letting it go practically, as so much of our usage
is. A study of pharisaism on its best side greatly clears the real Christian issue. And we have abundant documents for it in much current
religion which denounces pharisaism with freedom and effect.

count all things as dust that we may prize God's grace. These words are not banal. They contemplate a church of one article with all the rest in its bosom, and a theology which would only set forth the scientific implicates of grace. This is not mutilation, not minimism, but a redistribution of accent, organization, and proportion. We surely do not deny other doctrines when we rally on the doctrine of grace, which issues and organizes them all freely. Let this be the one article of every organized church, and let us have freedom for every position that does not make it impossible.

In so far as Christianity is doctrinal it has but this one doctrine, which contains all the rest in the germ. The revision of doctrine which we require is simply allowing grace to organize truth and adjust its perspective. Doctrines, indeed, do not save. There are no saving doctrines. We have no dogmas, or system of dogmas, delivered us full grown, like the first Adam, and redemptive, like the second. We have no doctrine which we can lift over bodily from the Bible. The Bible is not a manual of doctrine for all time. It is not its function to present us with finished theology. Its theology is not condensed, but germinal, not complete, but mighty.*

But if there are no saving doctrines, in the sense of doctrines that save, there is and must be a doctrine of salvation. And it is the doctrine of Christ's grace, of the gospel deed for the conscience. We cannot describe Christ as different from us only in degree and not in kind, simply because all we really get then is man's deed in Christ; it is not God's grace for man. And if Christ represent but the height of human achievement, we have no authority for man

---

*Doctrine does not come directly from the Bible. It comes indirectly through the faith and church the Bible makes. If the Bible were our doctrinal compendium it would need and lead to an infallible interpreter in a church; and so we reach Rome and its refusal of the Bible to its people.

or his thought. But if we are objectively right in our experience of God's grace in Christ, we have the source, test, and key to all theologies, and the condition of better theologies yet to be. Yes, better yet to be! We must take no step backward unless it be for the run to leap forward. The new Reformation idea of faith has not yet had its scope in this matter. The Reformation theology was mainly Catholic; it was the Reformation religion, its living faith, that made the new departure and carried in its bosom the new theology. The Reformation, in its fight for a gospel existence, had to take over, and leave with us, a great mass of Christian truth framed on the Catholic idea which the whole movement rose to destroy, namely, that the mind's assent to truth was a greater thing than the will's obedience to grace. The confusions of Protestantism today are due to the native incompatibility of these two positions—the supremacy of assent and the supremacy of faith. And our scheme of truth has not yet been thoroughly reorganized by the vital current of the evangelical experience. The theology of the Reformation is not yet quite subdued to the religion of the Reformation. Its belief does not duly express its faith. And why does the reconstruction hang back? Because the churches are complacently failing that religion, failing that Reformation idea, that revolutionary idea of faith as the answer to grace. They are still more concerned with pity than with faith. And as to faith they still make it too much the answer to truth. Or else they make it but the answer to love. And both these tendencies are those of Roman Catholicism. It is Catholic to worship orthodoxy stiffly with the old people. And it is Catholic to worship love joyfully with the young. The Protestant, the New Testament, idea of faith is the penitent worship with tears and spikenard, with shame and glory, of God's justifying grace. In Protestantism the foundation of all Christian theology has been and must be the antithesis of grace and sin, of gospel and law. The Reformers, like Melanchthon, said it was only when we realized this that we began to be intelligent Christians. The one central doctrine of grace has in it the promise and the potency of all the truth, love, joy, and sanctity that the future can demand from the Bible and the church.

6.　　Authority and Theology

The fascinating aspect of this essay is its prior date to the similar chapter in *The Principle of Authority*. Forsyth states the grand scope of that authority as having the ground of all things in the goal of all things. After first tracing the base of authority and its nature, he turns to Protestant theology. Protestant theology is as deeply founded on authority as is Catholic theology. Only the form is different. Catholic theology bases its authority on external assent, while Protestant theology requires "an obedience of response, not of assent." That authority Forsyth finds in history, not in human personality. It is the source of morality and the seal of authority for a race redeemed or lost.

✿　　✿　　✿

From the *Hibbert Journal*
IV (October, 1905)

I.

There is no question so deep and urgent at this moment as that regarding the seat of authority and its nature.* Man

---

*Many suggestions in the first part of this article I owe to Dr. Kaftan of Berlin.

is not man by his power rightly to reason, so much as by his destiny duly to obey. The question is grave enough at any time, but with the bond of control so relaxed as today it is; with the traditional creeds and sanctities so shaken; with the public mind so hungry and yet so poor, so interested and yet so distracted upon final problems; with the rising generation tutored in independence till, in an evil sense, the child is father of the man; and with the rising classes so ignorant of responsibility, affairs, history, or human nature—it is a question more urgent than ever. Criticism has established its right: is Christianity left with any positive authority? And the inquiry is all the more urgent the less it is felt to press amid the multitude of problems, passing and passionate, which fills an outworn age trying to narcotize with mere energies its moral fatigue.

The question will not bear to be lightly handled. It is deeply implicated in the nature of human progress; and the law of progress is that from the great deep to the great deep it goes. Only quackery assures us that, as we move onward, the answers to the great questions grow more simple, and that the litterateur is now, by the spirit of the age, in a better position to deal with the old enigmas than the philosopher or the historian. Simplicity is not the test of truth. It is not the badge of progress. The simple solutions are the most suspicious. There is much preaching of simplicity which is no more than a sop to spiritual indolence. The immediate affections are indeed always divinely simple. But to transfer these affections to the object of worship and the ground of existence, either without more ado or on the word of some saintly soul; to say that it is one of life's first and clearest simplicities to think of the ultimate reality as Father, and trust him as sons—is to trifle with the subject and with the heart. It is no sign of real progress to settle today by the prompt intuition of a genial but impatient heart

questions which have taxed on a time the greatest intelli-
gences of religion and of the race. The doves have indeed
got into the eagle's nest when pulpit poets, with more taste
for abstractions than faculty for reality, can blandly close
questions which Jonathan Edwards had much ado to stir.

It is in the region of theology that this greatest of questions must be fought out. It is there that all such questions
must be decided, if they are admitted to be real questions
at all. And in the region of Protestant theology this must be
admitted. For the question is hardly real, it is but leisurely
and academic, in a church whose decision has been, ever
since Duns Scotus, an ecclesiastical positivity in default of
a rational or evangelical base.

But it will be said, on the other hand, that even in Protestantism the question can hardly be real, because in Protestant theology there can be no real authority since the collapse of scriptural infallibility. Any authority that may be
set up is so inward and so subjective that it quickly becomes
individualist, modish, and decadent. And thus (it is said)
theology here becomes no science of reality, but merely a
science of religious phenomenology. It may discuss the idea
of God on the lines of psychology and history, but it has
nothing final to say on the reality of God or gospel. We
may explore and admire the consciousness of Christ so far,
but we are in no position to say anything authoritative about
his gospel. We may own the extraordinary spiritual influence
of his person, but we cannot dogmatize about his work.
The only thing approaching finality in Christianity is the
spirit of Christ. And "the spirit is the emanation of his consciousness" (Sabatier). Under that influence we find rest.
But is it more than rest? Is it not but a mood, a lenitive
for life? Is it reality? Is it life itself?

In this brief article it can be little more than stated, in
reply to such remarks, that for Protestant theology the authority is not so much the historic, or the ideal, or the spirit-

ual Christ as the moral, holy, historic gospel of the grace
of God in and through him and his cross. It is not Christ
as ideal, or as spiritually infectious, but Christ as redeemer.

II.

Protestant theology is founded upon authority as much
as Catholic. It starts from something given. It is not the
discovery of new truth so much as the unfolding of old
grace. Christian truth is as unchangeable in its being as
it is flexible in its action. Surely Christian truth is something
fixed. It is not just what every man supposes. Individualism
there is mental anarchy. There must be authority. And by
authority is meant something outside our personal opinion,
will, vision, inclination, or taste. It is something which takes
a place we never give. It imposes itself on us. It comes
with power. It compels submission and obedience as the
condition of weal, order, and progress. One form of it is
essential to family life, another to civic life. Another is the
source of all salvation. It is so in our personal religion.
Everything there turns on the obedience of faith to faith's
authority. Is our theology, then, to have a different foundation from our faith? Is faith submission to a positive God,
but theology submission to nothing? Is it mere opinion?
What scepticism, what a fatal schism in our soul and creed
that would be! Again, a church must have an authority of
some kind (if it be as low as the authority of a majority).
But if theology own no authority, the two fall hopelessly
apart, just as they would if theology had an authority but
the church had none.

"But," it will be persisted, "if theology have an authority
it can never be a science. For science is absolutely free, and
with an authority that is in contradiction. A free science
owns no authority?" Except, of course, the authority of the
facts it founds on; to say nothing of the axiom that we can

trust our faculties. "Oh yes, of course, that is different." But is it different? Is it not the very point? Theology founds on certain historic facts, on the one revealed fact of a gracious God in particular. It founds on a fact with a particular nature and power—on Christ and his cross, and the effect of the cross—as chemistry might found on the qualities and effects of things. The authority in theology is not external to the matter it works in. It is spiritual. It is inherent in the fontal fact, and connate to the soul. It belongs to the revelation itself as such, and not to any voucher which the revelation created, like a book or a church. It is an authority objective to us in its source, but subjective in its nature and appeal.

If we are not sure and clear about an authority for faith or thought, we can have neither church nor theology. But if faith has no church, it has no contact, no affinity, with society, and so religion is hostile to humanity. And if it has no theology, it has no relation with science. Religion is then even hostile to science, because a science of our religion is impossible. No religion is friendly to science if it disown a science of itself. The fundamental relation of faith to science does not depend on its attitude to physical science, or even to philosophy, but on its capacity for a science of itself. A religion that despises a theology declares war on science in the act. We may abjure any interest in theology. Instead of regarding it as a precious gift of God, and a necessary element in a great church and culture, we may look on it with amused but vulgar patience as the hobby of certain maundering minds, impractical and ineffectual. We may choose the better part, as we think, and bury our heads in the sand of practical activity. That is an excellent function of a church, but it is a poor foundation. It looks plausible, and wears the air of Christian business. But it is of Philistia, not of Israel. And it has no stay. The churches with a theology must carry the day. No theology, no church; and no church, no kingdom.

III.

Protestant theology is as much dependent upon authority as Catholic, but the form of it is different. We have something over our thought as commanding in its nature as the church or pope is for Catholicism—nay, more so. The great matter in Catholicism is Christian truth, Christian doctrine, Christian system. That is really its supreme object of faith. Faith means assent to certain truths supernaturally conveyed and guaranteed. They were conveyed by a revelation which included the standing guarantee of an infallible church. Revelation is the supernatural donation of theological dogma, secured for all time by a church fixed at Rome. Faith, of course, is always the answer to revelation, and corresponds to its nature and source; and here it is the acceptance of these truths from the church as their responsible voucher. The church takes the responsibility for them, and takes it off each member. So faith of that kind really means faith in the church and acceptance of its absolute authority. And wherever revelation is understood to consist of a body of truth we have the Catholic habit of mind, and, in the long run, the Catholic result in the way of church and pope. There is much of it in circles violently anti-popish. The enmity is a family quarrel. Orthodoxy means intellectualism. And as most people are not intellectual enough to deal with such truths, this means that they must leave them to experts. And Romanism is simply the greatest apotheosis on earth of the expert, the specialist, and his tyranny. It deifies* the specialist in sacramental grace and truth.

---

*In the Roman catechism the priests are described as *dii*, pars ii., cap. vii., quest. ii.

But orthodoxy is foreign to the genius of Protestantism where the supreme matter is not dogma but grace, and grace understood as the gospel, as God's redeeming act in history and not his sacramental action in nature. It is a revelation not to one side of the man, the intellect which grasps truth, nor to the subliminal man whose defective substance needs a sacramental food or drug, but to the whole moral man, whose need is forgiveness, redemption, and power. It claims from him a different kind of obedience from Rome's, namely, faith in the sense of personal conviction, personal surrender, and personal trust in a gracious God. It is an obedience of response, not of assent. It offers up the man as a will, and not as a mind. Faith becomes really religious. It means an acceptance of grace, not as the sacramental capital of the church, but as mercy, forgiveness, and redemption in a definitive act entering our experience. The authority is neither primal truth, developed dogma, nor chartered institution, but this act, power, and person with whom we have direct dealings. It is the gospel in the cross, conceived as the moral word and deed of God, and not as any human version or report of it.

The see-saw of the old supernaturalism and rationalism is interminable, because both started from the same fallacy, that the content of revelation is truth as statement or doctrine. The one found it in the Bible, demanding acceptance through an external guarantee of prophecy and miracle; the other found it in the reason, guaranteeing truths not necessarily different from Bible truth, but held on a different ground. It was really a question of the religious authority, vitiated in its discussion by the notion, still popular and fatal, that religion is a thing of beliefs rather than of faith and revelation, a matter of truth rather than grace. Both sides were enmeshed in the intellectualist conception of religion. And supernaturalism fell (as it always must fall) before rationalism through the contradiction that the gospel was essentially a doctrine, while yet it was withdrawn from the criticism of the understanding. The whole discussion enters another plane when we leave the intellectualist and preceptual notion of revelation behind us, and escape from the doctrinaire forms of religion to a religion of spiritual, ethical, and personal relations; when we escape from classic forms of belief and give scope to the romantic claims of direct feeling and original experience; when the fixity of an initial system gives way to the results of historical inquiry both as to the absoluteness of the original revelation in Christ's person and the relativity of its subsequent course in the church's thought. A conception of authority is reached which not only allows criticism but demands it—which is indeed the true nature of the Reformation as the action of the self-corrective and self-preservative spirit of the gospel. The absoluteness of Christianity is to be sought only in its gospel of grace: treated as the historic act of God for man's moral destiny, and not for his scheme of truth. The antithesis of supernaturalism and rationalism goes out of date in its old form. The gospel is no less critical of the past than creative of the future. The revelation in the cross of God's holiness is equally one of critical judgment and of creative grace.

There is then no authority for mere theological knowledge or statement. There are doctrines of salvation, but no saving doctrines. In a strict use of words, there is no such thing as saving truth. No machine ever sat or sits minting and issuing it as the one lawful currency for the Christian mind. And no formal gift of it was ever made to man, and put in the church's charge to keep undefiled. For the Protestant authority exists not in the theological form of dogma or statement, but in the evangelical form of historical grace, which is the soul and power of revelation. It is an authority truly religious. Our supreme good is not knowledge, not correct doctrine (which is a pagan perversion of Christianity caused by Greece, and loaded with intellectual

pride). It is a moral thing, and essentially holy. It means
more than a mystic union with the divine. It is the practical
obedience and penitent response of faith in the historic
grace of Christ to the conscience. The Christian gospel is
an authority for the will, in the will's sphere of history; it
is not for the intellect—except in so far as the intellect de-
pends on the will. It is an authority which is felt primarily
as authority, not as truth—as Christ was felt, not as the
Scribes. That is, it is morally realized, not mentally; per-
sonally, not officially; ethically, and not aesthetically, not
contemplatively. It is for conscience, not for thought, in
the first place, nor for imagination. It so settles the whole
moral man that in the region of truth there is entire flex-
ibility and freedom. We have the liberty there that rests on
final confidence and security. Certainty of living faith in
grace gives us liberty of thought in truth. To be sure, truth
is implicit and integral to Christianity, but it is not supreme.
Christ comes full of grace and truth, but with the grace
uppermost and always central. Grace represents the fixed,
fontal, authoritative, evangelical element; truth, the element
free, adjustable, and catholic. The one appeals to our personal life-conviction, the other to our scientific judgment.
We own the authority of grace by impression and not perception, by conviction and not observation, by life and not
by thought. It is in personal relation with us. It is the authority in it that breeds the knowledge, the science, the
theology. It is not the knowledge that is the ground of the
authority; it is the authority that is he ground of the knowledge (though, of course, in the empirical worder of time, the
knowledge may come first). There is assent as well as trust.
But the *fiducia* precedes the *assensus,* and produces it freely.
The freedom that is worth most to Christian theology is not
free thought but a free soul. It is not cosmic and rational,
but ethical, vital, evangelical. It is not the freedom of the

world's harmony, but the freedom of Christ's reconciliation, of free and freeing grace.

IV.

It is one of the fundamental mistakes we make about our own Protestantism to say that the authority is the conscience, and the Christian conscience in particular. Not so. The authority is nothing in us, but something in history. It is something given us. What is in us only recognizes it. And the conscience which now recognizes it has long been created by it. The conscience recognizes the tone of injunction, but what is enjoined is given by history, and has passed into the historic conscience. We have the inner intuition of what is a great historic teleology. It is not gathered up from all history by an induction, which, as history is far from finished, could never give us anything final or authoritative. But it is divined in it at a fixed point by faith in the experienced revelation of final purpose within God's act of gospel. The authority is not the conscience, but it is offered to it. The conscience of God is not latent in our conscience, but revealed to it in history. It is history, and not conscience, that is the real court of morals. And it is there accordingly that we find the authority for Christian faith and Christian theology, for faith and theology both. It is the glory of Protestantism that we have the same source and standard for both in the grace of God. That is the historic spring of both, and the constant measure of both. We have an external authority which is not foreign to the soul, yet not native to it. It is not mystic at the heart of man's depths; it is historic in the midst of man's career. Our theology rests on no other foundation than our religion. Our religion rests on a theological fact and its nature.

There is but one thing that corresponds to all the conditions of an authority: that is ethical, revealed, historic, personal, synthetic, and for ever miraculous to natural thought. There is one thing powerful over us forever, because forever marvellous and inexplicable, yet morally intelligible, beyond discovery, the very soul and essence of revelation. It is the grace of God toward human sin in Jesus Christ and his holy atonement. This is intelligible to no reason. It is for ever amazing. It is only taken home by living faith to moral need. It is the moral core and reality of the gospel that saves it from the sentimentalism that so easily besets it. Grace is not irrational in the sense of being foreign to reason, but it is not in the reason of it that its authority resides. There is nothing which is such a surprise, such a permanent surprise, and such a growing surprise to reason as grace; yet it is in the act and agent of grace that our moral experience finds authority at its final source, however seldom that source is visited by the soul or the society it controls.

"All that is absolute in the natural conscience is the sense of obligation. 'You *must* do what is right.' Yes, but it does not tell us what is right. That is the judgment of the reason according to circumstances. The real conscience of the conscience is the gospel. This not only brings absolute obligation but absolute right and truth. It not only satisfies the natural conscience, its forerunner, but it opens to it a new world, it provides a new ideal and standard which it guarantees as the final reality. It reveals in the conscience new needs, and raises it to appreciate the moral value and right of a doctrine like atonement, which to its natural light seemed strange and incredible" (note in Bertrand's *Redemption,* p. 494). There is absolutely no reason why God should forgive and redeem men. All the reason we know, apart from his own revelation of himself and his purpose, is against it. There is nothing we have less natural reason to expect, except in so far as reasonable expectation has been colored by the foregone revelation itself in the course of history. There is nothing, moreover, that so far passes human power as to forgive, in the deep, real, ultimate, divine sense of the word. As a revelation, grace is absolutely synthetic. It unites what it was beyond man's power to unite—sin, love, holiness, and judgment; and it unites them for ever in endless beauty and power, in the one object of faith and source of morals—the cross of Jesus Christ.

V.

The grace of God in the historic cross of Christ must be the one source of morals and seal of authority for a race that is redeemed or nothing, redeemed or lost. The greatest fact in social ethics is also the most formidable and intractable; it is the fact of sin and the sense of guilt. All morals are academic which fail to recognize this—the real royalty of the moral, its actual wreck, and its imperative redemption. Whoever masters that fact of sin masters the conscience, and so, through the primacy of the moral, the whole of human life. The redeemer from moral death is the seat of final authority for a moral humanity. Anything we believe about incarnation springs from our faith in redemption. Our final moral standard is the gospel of the cross with its ethical restitution of things. It was the eternal and immutable morality of holiness that was effectually established there for history and forever.

There are ultimately no ethics, therefore, but theological. The natural conscience, were it accessible, would certainly be an object of scientific interest. But, strictly speaking (as has already been hinted), in civilized communities today it does not exist. It is a mere abstraction of thought. What does exist is a historic product, deeply and permanently molded by the Christian ethic of sin and redemption which for two thousand years has been shaping European morals. The authority that lifts its head in the individual conscience rises in an area which is never found detached, but always closing a long historical development, whose influence we may feel in weight more than we can measure in extent. Every conscience we enterrogate has this long social history for its *prius,* and, indeed, its progenitor. And the solemnity of the moral world within each of us is the accumulated and condensed sanctity of centuries of belief, ages of conscience, and millions of wills bowed before the holy order and urgency which wakes human faith, or, if we break with it, makes human tragedy. What the historic student of the actual situation has to count with is either the Christian conscience in more or less definite form, or some reaction from it more or less indebted to it.

For practical purposes, upon the scale of all human life and of the whole, passionate, actual soul, we must deal with the evangelical conscience shaped by faith in the grace of God redeeming in Jesus Christ. That is the true and typical human conscience as things are. Sin is not an influence which affects but a sectional conscience, or troubles but a few members of the race. In so far as it is real at all, it affects and vitiates the whole conscience, the whole man, that is, and the whole race in its moral aspect and reliability. There is no such thing as a natural conscience giving the normal material for ethics, with a redemptive provision of a supplementary, religious, and corrective kind for those abnormal cases that have erred and strayed. In so far as ethical science proceeds on such a basis it is meager and scholastic, and draws too little on the religious experience in history for an adequate or sympathetic account of human nature. For the actual moral life of the race as we find it to our hand forgiveness has the place of a constitutive principle, and not of an accident or supplement.

Redemption, taken in earnest, is critically constructive for the whole man and for all men. It is not a mere contribution to the future, but its one condition, not to say creation. It makes a new conscience for the race, with an authority seated in the source of the new creation—in the grace and gospel of God in Christ's cross. The principles of the new and normal conscience are drawn from the nature of that cross, from its moral theology, from its revelation of holiness, and not from any intuitions of natural goodness, or even of Christian piety. If (by such an admission as Huxley's) it is only by something in the nature of a miracle that humane ethics arise out of cosmic order, it is but lifting the statement to a higher plane by historic sense when we say that the conscience of the new race rests on the moral miracle in the cross. And it is but a corollary of the same when we say that it is in the forgiver and redeemer of the cross that the seat of moral, and so of all, authority for the renovated race must be found. The ethics of the future must be the explication of the holiness in the cross, and the obedience of the future must be to the Christ of the cross. The holy is the moral authority. And the supreme revelation of the holy is in the harmonized judgment and grace of the cross, at once critical and creative for the whole of society. The faith which answers that and is made by it is the moral marrow of the race. The seat of authority is the seat of the gospel. It has always been where mankind found the power of God; and it must increasingly be where sinful man finds the power of a holy God for salvation. And experience finds this but in Christ and in his cross, in the victories achieved thereby in our own life, and the conquests gathered from the evangelization of the world.

VI.

To all ethics drawn from real life the great human soul is lamed and doomed by the malady of sin. We struggle not only with misfortune nor with fate, but with some curse. And the total and ultimate moral situation of the race is thus not moral only, but religious. The malady and the remedy are religious both. The Lord of the race is not simply the genius of excellence, nor "a self-transcending goodness," even when that goodness is viewed as a personal ideal. He is a redeemer, who not only *embodies* goodness for our gaze, but *enacts* it for our salvation; who not only startles us with the wonder and love of our ideal selves, but *intervenes* with his goodness in redemptive action as the only condition of our power to fulfill ourselves, appreciate his revelation, or share his life; who not only reveals his kingdom, but *establishes* it in moral and historic reality.

But he is especially king and lord when we realize *how* he became redeemer, and what is the nature of his saving act. His authority does not rest simply on our grateful sense of the fact. That experience is too subjective and unstable for a seat of authority spiritual, absolute, and eternal. It is not simply that he produces on us the aesthetic impression of one in whom all human goodness foreruns itself, and all the soul's moral future is set forth by anticipation as an ideal to man and a pledge to God. It is not alone that we are melted and mastered by the spectacle of his grace. The seat of his eternal authority is neither in our wonder, fascination, nor gratitude. He rules neither as ideal nor as helper. His throne has a deeper and more objective base. He satisfied for us that holy law which our worst sin could never unseat, against which the most titanic human defiance breaks in vain. He even becomes for us that self-satisfying law. He has taken over in his person all the lien held upon our conscience by all the moral order of the world, all the holy righteousness of God. By his perfect obedience, his acceptance of holy judgment, his perfect fulfillment and satisfaction of God's holiness, he is identified with it. He becomes the reversionary, therefore, of all its claims upon the race. By his perfect satisfaction* of God's holiness, he

*By satisfaction is meant no equivalency of penalty, but adequacy of practical recognition. The idea is qualitative and not quantitative.

becomes the trustee of it for God among men. Because he took man's judgment he became man's judge. There is a close inner unity between sacrifice and judgment. "The saints shall judge the earth"; and the saints are such by their relation to sacrifice. The supreme sacrifice is in principle the final judgment, and the supreme victim the last judge. He who absorbed the curse and dissipated it acquires the monopoly of human blessing. And he who met the whole demand of holiness with his person becomes the law's Lord, in as far as holiness is above mere righteousness. So by the nature, and not by the mere fact and impress, of his work for us he becomes our king—the conscience of the conscience, himself the living and holy law which is our moral ultimate. He is thus the fountain of moral honor, and the center of moral authority, forever and for all. He would indeed be supreme if our orderly moral nature were only constituted in him; he is more profoundly and vitally supreme because our disordered nature is in him redeemed.

VII.

It is easy to anticipate an objection which arises to the line of thought here pursued. It is an objection too congenial to the spirit of the age to be easily overlooked; indeed, no one is quite equipped for dealing with this whole subject if it has not arisen in his own thoughts, and been not only laid as a specter of the mind but fought as a recalcitrancy of the will. There is a tendency to dwell in a region where it seems narrow to personalize, immodest to define, and overbold to be as positive or ethical about spiritual process as a word like redemption implies. There are few who have not felt at least the germs of that common reluctance to submit thought to the personal category, and will to a personal control. And there are many, not unspiritual, who never overcome their repugnance to accepting redemption as the fundamental note of the religious and moral life. Redemption in their case, like personality in the case of others, seems to imply a limitation of thought and an archaism of belief. It claims in the redeemer an exclusiveness of authority, and a uniqueness of nature, foreign to modern views of religious science, of human progress, and of personal independence. Like the pessimists, they will more readily admit a redemptive process than reduce it to the act of a redeemer. And while they believe in a divine humanity, it seems an indignity to condense it and submit it to the absolute authority of any one that arose in its midst.

But for the purposes of religion it is power that we need more than breadth; it is control as the condition of freedom; it is height, depth, and quality of soul more than range; it is security more than progress, and divinity more than fraternity. The passion of inclusion has overreached the soul's own comprehensive power; and we are losing real width of vision because our leveling instincts have robbed us of the commanding heights. There is a narrowness like that of the mountain peak which raises us much more than it limits us, and increases our range while it straitens our steps. To be just to mankind is not to be diffuse in our loyalties, grudging towards an elect, or cold in our worship of a unique. "To be just," says Baudelaire, "criticism must be partial and passionate, with a point of view which is exclusive indeed, but which opens new horizons." And another says, "L'amour, c'est choisir." It is so with regard to our moral critic, judge, and Savior. The eternal equity is partial to us. The moral universe is not a windless vacuum. It is too full of holy passion to leave room for absolutely impartial (and impossible) judgments, whether in man or God. The judge after all is just—because he is on our side, a just God and a Savior. And we cannot be just unless we are on his.

Personality and partiality are here but the concentration

so essential for conviction and power. The lack of certainty today is not only due to the many things and the many points of view, but still more to the weakness of will which refuses to select and concentrate. Much more doubt is voluntary and culpable than it is the fashion to admit. The mental confusion is due to some moral weakness and discursiveness. It is not wholly mental error, but to some extent moral dullness (to say the least), which causes so many to pass over the historic Christ as lightly as they do in their survey of the field of fact. There is a lack of moral insight and of moral perspective due to an absence of moral culture. We have come to a time when it is the element of command rather than comprehension that we need in our faith. And for this end a person has more power than a process, and a redeemer than an ideal. We may or may not be "broad," but positive and objective we must be. We may or may not be "liberal," but we must have liberty. And the first condition of positiveness in our creed, or freedom in our soul, or liberty in the state, is a sure, clear, personal and historic authority whose writ runs to the very center of the will and the recesses of the soul. The present decay in the matter of public liberty and its vigilance is more than concurrent with the decay of sure faith in a divine authority.

7. The Cross as the Final Seat of Authority

This essay urges a conversion upon some of the church's own ideas. The word *evangelical* needs especially to be converted. Forsyth's call for self-reformation appeals to the Reformers of the 16th century and to Martin Luther in particular. The gospel is superhuman rather than supernatural.

> And we must insist on the New Testament idea of the *miraculous nature of the Christian life,* whether *we* entered on it by a sudden breach with our past or not.[1]

What is needed is far more a gospel of authority than a gospel of freedom. "Without a real authority Protestantism is not only a blunder, but it deserves to be a failure." The release of the gospel from wrong views of the Bible is what Protestantism has that can confront the dogma of papal infallibility.

> Both Bible and church may be the means of our faith, but neither is the ground of our faith. . . . The Reformation was not the rediscovery of the Bible chiefly, but of the gospel in the Bible.[2]

---

[1]*Contemporary Review* LXXVI(1899), p. 591 and below.
[2]*Ibid.,* p. 604.

Forsyth here explains the nature of that gospel which alone is the religion of Protestants.

❊   ❊   ❊

From the *Contemporary Review*
LXXVI (October, 1899)

I.

In converting the world, the church should not forget that there are conversions to be brought about within her own pale, and especially upon some of her own ideas. The self-reformation of the church is not merely an event of the sixteenth century; it is the church's standing instinct of self-preservation amid the corruptions and errors of history; it is a permanent condition of the church's health, and an exercise of the vital spirit whose indwelling makes it a church and keeps it so.

And it is a great part of the church's duty today to convert, perhaps the idea, but certainly the word, *evangelical.* It needs restoring from its fallen to its first state. It needs to be rescued from the sects and restored to its public and universal scope. It is time that it changed its meaning in the public mind from a symbol of the narrow and the stale to the whole breadth of the soul, the whole depth of the human tragedy, and the whole tension of the human crisis —the soul's crisis and the social need. It is urgent that more should be done to dissociate the word from the theories of grace and to attach it to the realities of grace; to adjust it at once to the historic Christ and to the historic and actual situation of society. It needs to be moralized, to become more ethical and more practical. It requires to be adjusted to Christ and to social need more even than to the Bible.

It is desirable that we should realize the evangelical authority to be not so much the Bible as the gospel, the Bible in the Bible and before it, the gospel of grace and redemption in the person of Christ, the Bible's living spirit to be distilled from it, not its dead residuum to be obtained by evaporation or dissection.

We ought to be as evangelical as our fathers, especially as our early fathers of the Reformation. But what does that mean? It means that we should fit grace to need, and be as relevant with a gospel of grace to our age as they were to theirs. For instance, we are many of us living on the evangelical revival of the last century. That was a great and a timely movement. It was a movement against spiritual deadness in the church. And its protest has been not only effective but vital. It saved the church, and it continues to do so: that deadness does not now exist. The church is quick and powerful, and it would be a mistake to suppose that the evangelical testimony is today called on to take the same form. To repeat the old phrases and experiences may (I do not say must) savor of insincerity or of unintelligence. Revival is not now the need of the church, at least in the same sense. The social situation is different, and the church's mood is different. The great Protestant movement has passed into another phase, and the Protestant principle asserts itself in another and more relevant form.

It is still the old watchword of grace to human sin and faith. But there are at least two points on which the Christian situation of the day calls for special stress:

1. Grace today must be a gospel not so much of the supernatural as of the superhuman; it needs to be preached as transcending human love even more than natural law.

2. And as it is thus much more than sympathy, so it must be a gospel not in the first place of freedom, but of authority.

I venture to say something on the first of these heads, but most on the second.

1. Our gospel is superhuman, even more than supernatural.

The word and thought of the supernatural are very largely due to the eighteenth century, with its idolatry of nature, not only in the science which this century has popularized, but in the literary movement associated with such names as Rousseau, Wordsworth, and Burns. For the hour it is the literary movement that holds the field. What fills the air today is not nature, but humanity. What creates difficulty is not so much historic miracle as human misery. There is a rebound from the objective to the subjective. The ruling note is not law but love, not the head but the heart, not science but literature: and literature not of the classic sort, but of the sort that makes direct appeal to the most untutored sentiments, to the sentiments which are ready rather than great. The note is humanism native or refined: whereas the gospel, if it remain a matter of grace and not of course, must be superhuman. The literary man is not a priest except in a literary and unreal sense. Last century the church had to protect grace against a rational humanism; this century it faces a sympathetic humanism; we confront at once a vaster rationalism in idealism, and a more winsome humanity in aestheticism. Our fathers had to assert grace in a Christendom which believed in law and reason; we have to do it in a world, and even a church, which believes chiefly in love and pity. Faith then was to see grace as love; now it is to see love as grace. Then God's grace needed interpreting as love; now God's love needs interpreting as grace. Then the cross needed interpreting by love; now love needs interpreting by the cross. Faith is not the response to love, but to grace; it is not Christian sympathy, but Christian repentance.

The forms of humanism are the aesthetic (or literary) and the philanthropic, and each by itself threatens the evangelical note. Each would detach love and pity from the moral conditions of sin, and therefore from grace. Each would naturalize Christ's love, and, while enhancing its charm, would reduce its miracle. Each would make religion but the spiritualized man, natural affection etherealized.

But to love your enemy and forgive your revilers is a totally new and supernatural affection. It is not a natural affection educated, cultured, and refined. Our note is neither culture nor is it character as the result of culture—even of religious culture. It is the change made by grace as an act of forgiveness, and not as a system of consecration. Christianity needs to some extent to be saved from its own moral success, from a monopoly by those who have been "born good," and reared in the fine law of Christian purity, love, and consideration. And Christianity is the only religion that can both produce such characters and save itself from being captured and trimmed down even to their delicate legalism.

We cannot, perhaps, insist, as our free church fathers did, on purity of communion, secured in individual cases by a scrutiny which to many would now seem indelicate, not to say harsh. But we can make it the more of an ideal as we make it the less of a test. And we must insist on the New Testament idea of the *miraculous nature of the Christian life,* whether *we* entered on it by a sudden breach with our past or not. Its nature is a standing break with the world in the sense that there is for the soul a decisive difference between the human graces as evolved from nature and as devolved from grace.

One of our chief difficulties when we speak of a gospel of grace rather than of love is the shallowness of the public mind and conscience, its passion for immediacy, its sensibility to the interests of the hour, its impressionism. The kind of thoughts and doubts which prevail in religion belongs to the light of nature and the literary class. It is the pain and waste in nature that suggest question of a God; it is the impulses of the heart that indicate him. Faith stands or falls by natural sentiment. Some of the booklets that sell by thousands on great themes are not the work of the real thinkers or saints, but of men who have the knack of writing chapters from the rambling heart-history of the intelligent man in the street. The amateurishness, not in thought only, but in experience, on the part of those novelists who hold public attention on some of the great themes is very offensive—as is also a certain jaunty air of pioneers, while they are only turning, and not even threshing, the old, old straw. The serious thinkers are discredited as ponderous pedants, and there is a cant against theology or theological religion. But religion must be either theological or sentimental, and if it is sentimental its life is brief. It has no depth of earth. Christianity was theological and not literary at the first. The theologians are simply the competent in their kind. And while we do not wish to consecrate systems, we do need the guidance of the competent.

Let us educate our ministers. But do not let their education wait for their professional experience. They should be in a better educated position before they begin to educate. And let us not do it by the press. If ministerial training is not wholly training by blunders, no more is it by courses of novels, essays, and newspapers. Nor is the idol of the press the ideal of the church. Much nonsense is spoken about learning to know the heart. That is not the minister's first business, which is to know his gospel. The gospel brings with it that knowledge of the heart which stands the preacher in best stead. There is more humanism in the gospel than there is gospel in humanism, more literature in the Bible than Bible in literature.

The gospel of grace is superhuman as well as supernatural; it is as much above natural affection as above natural law. The central act of grace is as much beyond the natural heart to do as it is beyond the natural reason to explain. It is a revolution more than an evolution. What is at our Christian center is more of a miracle than of a law, an idea, or a passion.

Need I say that no word is to be raised against either literature or philanthropy? They are just as necessary to life as faith is, and a living faith which takes hold of the social order is bound to develop them. A caution is only required when their principles and tests are made the final standard of faith, and the Christian revelation of grace is required to plead at the bar of culture or benevolence for its right to command men or its claim to bless them.

2. But what I desire chiefly to say is this. A gospel of grace should come to the church and society of today more as a gospel of authority than as a gospel of freedom.

I do not say that it should come *first* in that form. It need not begin on the keynote. But the keynote should be as I say. Sympathy and freedom are the language of the time, and we must speak that language to be understood. But what the language must convey is a gospel which, in its nature, is the very authority for soul and conscience that the age chiefly needs.

The air is full of freedom. We have more freedom than we know what to do with. Without a clear charter it becomes to many a misery. This was not the case one hundred years ago even. The great political and social victories of the century have placed us in a totally new position. We have realized two things in particular—a sense of individual freedom and a sense of responsibility for our brother. Yes; but responsibility to whom or to what? On that head we are not so clear. What we need is a power that rules our freedom because he gives it, and a power that accepts and sustains our sacrifice because he inspires it. We need supremely an obedience.

The question of the hour, and still more of the future, is as to the true and final seat of authority.

There is no question so deep and urgent if we will but hear it. It is momentous enough at any time, but it is more pressing now than ever amid the dissolution of so much that used to pass without question and to be obeyed without demur. It is a question, too, not of church organization, nor of political forms, nor of coherent creeds, but of the very cohesion of society itself. The bond of control is everywhere relaxed, and there is a recrudescence of faith in those forceful, primitive, and external methods of coercion which can extort no more than a sullen submission from our awakened and awakening time. We succed better with the organizing of society than with the unifying of life. "Fehlt leider auch der geist'ge Band." The traditional creeds and sanctities are shaken; reverence is more aesthetic and formal than really obedient. The rising generation is tutored in independence for its own sake till the child is in the unloveliest sense the father of the man. The rising classes are unfamiliar with history, with experience, with responsibility, human nature, or affairs. The public mind is unready for its own future; it is interested yet distracted upon final problems. The sense of a real authority is not growing so rapidly as the sense of the unreality of what has served as authority. And there is both in the intellectual and the spiritual world an aversion which amounts to impatience towards the spiritual effort and insight for which the real situation calls. The very ethical interests of the hour are not searching except in a few; and they find it difficult to secure a hearing except in plays or tales which do more to reveal the pain than to heal the disease. They raise "ghosts" that they cannot lay.*

This question of the final seat of authority is not yet

---

*Since the above was written I have lighted on the following, which I translate from Eucken's "Grundbegriffe der Gegenwart," p. 315: "Viewed as a whole, the present time shows on the central problems much reflection but little insight. It knows much but it creates little. It has many interests but small power, plenty of elasticity but poor faculty for following out fixed and independent principles. In a word, it has plenty of talent but little character. It lacks spiritual substance, and with that the feeling for the substantial, the faculty to distinguish the real from the apparent, the sound from the sick. So we have a huge contrast between our tireless, capable, and fertile work in the *breadth* of things and our total vacuity when it is a question of life in its *depth* and life as a whole."

earnestly faced by Protestantism. We are still misled by the notion that Protestantism is chiefly valuable as a protest against authority in favor of the rights of an individual or a minority. But without a real authority Protestantism is not only a blunder, but it deserves to be a failure. We need an authority more than anything else; and it is the offer of what seems a real authority that is the very life of the anti-Protestant theories of the church and the Counter-Reformation. We shall not hold society for Protestantism unless we can make good an authority more real and more searching than the imposing, spiritual, and subtle authority whose seat is at Rome.

II.

With the Reformation entered the new age of European culture, the modern mind. By this is not intended culture on its academic or its aesthetic side. That dawned in the Renaissance. What is meant is not *Bildung* but *Kultur,* not merely refinement but progress, not simplicity but complexity, not education so much as civilization. It might sound pedantic to say that with the Reformation there burst upon Europe the modern consciousness, but it would be more accurate. Of this consciousness the most striking feature is the universal and passionate assertion of individual freedom and its contents. The general mind has become subjective to a degree never realized in the previous history of the world. We have arrived at the very egoism of humanity, and even its apotheosis. Men are such units as they never were before; but also never was man so much to man. "Man," says Herder, "has no nobler word for his destiny than he himself *is.*" Even the humanism of Greece never made man such an actual power in his world. The great chorus in the "Antigone" is long outdone. For, while there has gone with this modern subjectivism some measure of the weakness of introspection and sentiment, it has carried with it much more of control over the world, and much more sense of a right to its conquest. The new inwardness is matched by the new outwardness. We cannot, indeed, say that modern civilization has overcome the world in the finest and most solemn sense of these words. For there are many signs that the world has seduced the soul of its conqueror and shorn his immortal strength away. The spiritual cowardice of their agnosticism is a singular comment on the bold mastery of the outward world shown by the progressive and Protestant races. But it remains true that the modern mind is marked by a sense of itself which is as unprecedented as its sense of the world. It is objective in its intelligence and subjective in its passion. The perilous, the fatal thing is that the objective which it feels most is cut off (also in an unprecedented degree) from anything in its nature authoritative. What we know is nothing by which we are known. Our research leaves us with no feeling that we are searched and tried. Our confessions of ignorance grow with our growing knowledge, but they do not leave us humble. The universe cows our mind, but we take it out in a subtler pride. And so we have the chemist, the explorer, and the engineer of the day balanced on their spiritual side by an overweening selfhood represented by Nietzsche. *Das Uebermenschliche* gives way to his *Uebermensch*. The Titan among men claims the same right to beat their morals under his feet as titanic man has to lord it over the immense world he can range. The world has swelled both *in* man and *for* man, but its growth *for* man has lost in authority what it has gained in extent; therefore the world *in* man has lost its poise, and he becomes his own drunken god and most accomplished Trinculo.

Yet the main course is right. It was inevitable that man should be forced upon that spiritual selfhood which the Reformation brought and perilled on the edge of his individual freedom. No obedience is sound which is not free. The world had long worked in upon him. As nature or as empire, as paganism or Catholicism, it had crushed the soul. It was quite necessary that he should turn and work outward on the world. If the soul was as eternal as the church had declared it to be, it was bound to realize that it was in command of time, which was at most but a part of eternity. But if of time then of history; and if of history then of an historic church. The soul claimed the right to revise the church, and judge the church, and condemn it—yea, reject it. It could by grace educate its master. If the destiny of the soul was everything, it must surely take its true place one day even over the pedagogic institutions which had taught it its royal worth. It is true that the downfall of the old authority left it in a naked and perilous state. The infant self could not but feel in course of time the chill and terror of its new and imperial solitude. The *pædagogia puerilis,* from which Melanchthon said Luther had freed the church, was outgrown only in principle. Even today the release is still far from an actual and complete one, and we have masses of people, increased by the *debut* of women on public and *direct* influence, who are psychologically in the Middle Ages still. They flee shivering into the soft, warm air of a church climate subtropical if not torrid, clerical if not priestly, in its prescriptions, guidance, and claims. How could it be otherwise? "The monk is always a minor," and the priest tends to be a dwarf. It was a too long tutelage that these exercised in Europe—longer than our three centuries even can yet outgrow. Europe had been immersed in a spiritual *lycée* till its powers and passions were a man's while its soul remained largely a child's. Such things are but slowly repaired. With the unity of the church disappeared the power which for a thousand years had been not only an outward authority but an outward authority of a very inward kind. An institution like that cannot be plucked from the mind that it has so long made without a shock, and a shock which can only be steadied by an authority greater still. And where was that to be found? There was nothing on earth that could claim it; no body had been slowly prepared for it. It could not be transferred. Authority is not easily transferred; it must grow. The new churches could not claim it, at least in the sense of the old. They arose from a breach of church authority, they bore the stamp of their origin, and it was not far that they could go in any authoritative claim. So they strove to fall back on two things. They fell back on the authority of the civil power which made the church at last the flat appendage of the state that it is in Germany and England today. And they fell back upon the Bible. But what was the Bible? The church had put it there—as a canon at least; and the church had claimed to interpret it ever since. If another interpretation was offered it must be the result of private judgment and sectional experience. At least, it could not impress itself upon the outer world or against the church with any greater weight than a personal experience gave. Protestantism, when the glow of its first mighty impulse had cooled, found itself in a condition of spiritual anarchy, which is our dread inheritance and our supreme but not insoluble problem. The Roman church has not ceased to go forward in the line of its magnificent and unholy audacity. The dogma of papal infallibility has in it something sublime in its self-certitude, to which we can no more refuse a certain aesthetic admiration than we can to Milton's Satan. What has Protestantism with which to confront that, still more bold, commanding, and thorough? The disintegration of the Bible, say some cynics. No; but the release of the gospel from wrong views of the Bible; the growing consolidation of a great evangelical church, which the sects do not distract but enrich. The gospel, and the gospel alone, is the religion of Protestants.

One thing is sure. We can never solve that problem by the silly device of overleaping the Reformation and picking up the medieval state of things. Such could only be the view of an archeologist and not an historian, of a cleric and not a prophet. We have, in the teachable part of us at least, learned that history demands a treatment much more informed, respectful, and modest than that. The way from medievalism *could* only lie forwards through the Reformation. It is not for nothing that these great movements of the spirit take place. And this movement took place to much greater purpose than merely to produce a Counter-Reformation and present the world with the Council of Trent. The Reformation struck into the right path. Authority could only be replaced by a religious way. It must remain religious. A religious authority could never be replaced by one merely rational, political, or individual. A living and present church must only be superseded by something equally living and near. And the religious way must lie through the subjective realm. Whatever could be done by a religious authority chiefly outward had been done. The new universal could only be found in the soul's interior, in the soul being forced inward and downward upon itself. If there be no universal and final imperative there, there is none anywhere. The Reformation took an indispensable step, a step that the best work of the church had made inevitable, when Luther transferred the supreme problem of life to the area of the personal conscience. And though the awful scope of the problem might burst and break the individual soul in the conflict, yet it was in these very ruins that the new life and the new reign arose. The new creation must begin from the soul's chaos and night. Whether you take Peter, Paul, or the Lord of both, the new man arises from a broken man, the new church from a broken church, and the victory of faith is on the field of blood. Revolution is an idea more central to the church's gospel than evolution. The spiritual conflict which had hitherto been waged by the church as a whole, and softened indefinitely for the individual, had left him, by this consideration for his weakness, too weak to face the world. At least he was unfit to face the terrors of a spiritual world, and the church could no longer fortify him. The whole moral tragedy of the world was now active into the arena of the single soul and its resources. The soul no less than the faith, the gospel, had come to the dilemma which stakes the whole future upon an "either—or"; and it is upon the decision that the decided make that the gentler and milder, the more harmonious and less thorough souls unwittingly live. So the self-complacency of the soul, yea, its very self-respect, was annihilated; and it was shut up into the new authority of a direct and personal *redeemer*. A helper was useless. The true Paraclete means much more than that. Ideals but mocked and damned. The soul was driven into such a corner of its interior that the outward had no worth for it except as a miracle—a creative miracle of rescue and grace. It so sank into itself that it could only rise redeemed—not refreshed but rescued. The medieval idea of a progressive salvation and gradual incorporation of the human with the divine was driven out by a complete revolution and a saving catastrophe. The pelagian and educational idea of salvation was displaced by a decisive and divine intervention. The development of natural goodness or of baptismal grace was no longer the type of salvation, but the radical change effected in personal faith. Sanctification could not be so directly and deliberately worked at without the blight of self-consciousness. Seek first for the kingdom and sanctification will be added; care for Christ and he will take care of your soul; sail by the cross and you will sail into holiness. Religion became much more miraculous than evolutionary; but it was a miracle worked on the will, and not on the nature or substance of the man. And within the soul's agonized extremity there was revealed the new authority in the moral form and nature of an absolute and universal redeemer. Christ become the new conscience and the new king. The cross and not the church becomes the new seat of his

authority—the cross as Christ crucified afresh in the evangelical experience of the desperate soul, and rising anew in
its new trust and new life.

By such individualism, individualism was in principle
destroyed. In the extremity of personal concern, belittle-
ment, and despair, arose a life which was a world in itself.
The redeemer was also the kingdom. To the soul he "became its universe that sees and knows." And a church of
those who are in Christ took the place of a church of the
baptized. A Christ who placed men in a church took the
room of a church that placed men in Christ. Such is the
principle which as yet, however, Protestantism has but half
actualized. That great movement has fallen under the fate
that befell Christianity itself before it was 200 years old. It
has been captured by culture, by another freedom than the
redeemed, by another subjectivity than the sanctified. It
has become identified with natural and civil progress
through friction, with the rejection of all authority, with the
assertion of a native independence whose ideal is the healthy
stalwart who never knew what it was to stand in the presence of a superior. There is much that attracts the raw
young mind in the manly ideal of an insubordinate rough-
rider who can take a tender turn as hospital-nurse. The uni-
form of the trained nurse and the red garibaldian shirt are
indeed perhaps the badges by which the democracy of this
age might most expressively be symbolized to posterity. And
our very churches are more familiar with the idea of giving
free scope to the individual and to the young than with the
prior and primary obedience of faith as a real act of will
and person. The first demand now made of anything that
offers itself to faith is not that it shall be the clear will of
God according to his one revelation in Christ, but that it
shall commend itself to the heart. And by the heart is not
meant what Melanchthon or Schleiermacher meant by the
word, but something which is the joint product of literary

and domestic culture, the humane sympathies, and especially the atmosphere of the religious poets of the second rank and the poetic preachers of the first. There is no doubt of the charm of this frame of mind; and Protestantism has arrears to make up in the way of winsomeness. But it is doubtful if even art can live upon charm alone; and it is certain that faith cannot. And it suffers less at last from the absence of immediate sympathy than from the lack of immediate and absolute authority. If Protestantism has failed at all, it is as an obedience; and in so far it has failed to realize its own idea of redemption. For the first claim of an absolute redeemer is property in the redeemed, and absolute control in the first place of their wills and lives. It was faith in this sort that was Christ's constant quest; his demand for affection came second, and could only be met through the more radical faith.

May I here briefly recapitulate what I propose to say in reply to the questions which are raised by our historic spiritual situation?

The real and final seat of authority is evangelical. It is the cross of Jesus Christ. Neither soul nor society knows anything as a final authority but him crucified. The sovereign and the cement of society is the Savior of the soul. That rules man which rules the conscience; and that rules the conscience which forgives it and redeems. The conscience is not the ruler, but only the ruler's throne. The center of authority is the world's central moral act, which is the expression of the world's central moral personality and order. It is the act of redemption. It is not the ideal but the redeemer of the conscience that is its king. The cross is the seat of moral empire and human unity. There is more unanimity among the saved about the cross than there is among the enlightened about truth. The believer has an authority for society that the thinker has not. The church, when it has become truly reformed in its grasp of its gospel, will exercise a power among men denied to the schools. To redeem the conscience is to command society. A sinful humanity is shut up to obey its Savior. The cross did not in the first place lay down a law, announce a truth, or provide an ideal; but it did give practical effect once and for ever to God's miracle of grace. It therefore displaces the Bible, the church, the reason, or the heart as the final authority for human thought, life, and liberty. The authority that rules even the Bible is the gospel for whose sake the Bible exists. By the evangelical seat of authority it will be seen I do not mean the authority that has been invoked by evangelicalism, but the authority that is given in the nature of the gospel.

We may say, therefore, that the gospel of grace has this task before it today when we contrast it with its work a century ago. It has to relax its pressure upon thought and knowledge—especially regarding its own history in the world —and it has to increase its pressure on life. It has to sit more loosely to the organization of a creed, and press more heavily for the organization of society. It has to recast creeds, but it has still more to recast society. It has not only to reconstrue the love of God, but to reconstruct society by it, reorganize it into society. It has to move saving interest from the center of a theological to the center of a personal and social system. It prescribes a more informed theological freedom, and a more searching moral and social obedience. It offers more room for heresies and less room for schisms, whether as church sects or as social classes. We have been over-engrossed with the breaches between thinkers, scholars, and churchmen; we have now to repair the breaches between classes and between souls. We have slowly, wisely, and indirectly to import into the social world the principles of the brotherly church; and the tough colossal egoism which has been pruned and curbed in the spirit-world of repentance must not seek compensatory scope in the social or industrial world. But the obedience and serviceableness learned in the one must be carried into the other. The communion of saints must become the brotherhood of man; there is no other real meaning in the kingdoms of this world becoming the kingdoms of our God and of his Christ. The conversion of the human soul must mean, in the long run, the conversion of the social and industrial organization to the uses and principles of the soul. The same God who drew human society out of wild nature by ages of evolution must out of human society draw the kingdom of Christ. And the agent of this change is the miraculous gospel, more miraculous than the appearance of self-consciousness in the evolutionary scale. And the principle of the gospel is the final and irresistible authority to bend to this end the unruly passion of human self-seeking and self-will. It is one authority, theological or social. That which regulates what we believe inspires and prescribes what we are to do.

III.

I am to commend my case that the final seat of authority for human society is in the cross of the forgiver and the redeemer; that Christ is king, not as the Son of our creator, or as the logos of the reason, but as our Savior.

1. The seat of authority must be sought in the ethical direction rather than in such quarters as would usually be understood as rational. It is only in the practical reason that we find authority; the pure reason has none. There is no truth that we may not criticize; but there is such a person. There is no absolute formal truth, only an absolute person and his act. Science, even theology in so far as it is scientific, owns no truth as final. The absolute is the only final authority, and we touch that by the moral act of personal faith alone. Man is the free creature even more than the rational; the lower animals are more rational than free. And it must be in the region of his distinctive freedom that his king

resides; it is there he needs and finds his authority. It exists for free will rather than for free thought. For knowledge and thought there may be order and limit, but there is no authority, which, in the real, absolute, and final sense, exists for man as moral and not as intellectual. We receive from it our salvation, but not our creed. The truth as it is in Jesus is Jesus as truth. Revelation was in its essence redemption, an exercise of power rather than persuasion, and the gift of life rather than of truth. The remade man makes his truth out of the new gift of reality, as Paul did. The absolute authority of truth as truth means a reign of orthodoxy which has been one of the calamities of the church. It is but the rational side of that institution worship which, in the larger form of Catholicism, has made the church one of the perils of the Word.

The seat of authority must be primarily ethical, and act on the reason only ethically and indirectly. Our great response is an obedience more than an assent, and our strength is not so much certainty as trust. Our prime need is to know not so much where we have inquired, but in whom we have believed.

2. This ethical authority cannot be merely individual in its action; it must be social: morality has no meaning except through a society. Its word is not for the single conscience, but for the public. Its destination is not a group of wills, but the race. The Lord of the soul is the Lord of society. A single soul could not be a soul, nor have an eternal Lord. The ruler of a single conscience only would soon cease to rule even that conscience. My king would not for ever seem to me royal if he were king only of me. Right for me would lose its right over me if it were not right also for a world of me's. A God who is God only of individuals soon becomes an individual God. We relapse into theism, which is just individualism obtruded into God. There is no social authority possible on a mere theistic basis. The individual force of

moral authority is due to its social nature and power, to its seat in a God who is in his nature social, and in his unity manifold, triune. "L'Esprit Saint c'est Dieu social."

The seat of authority is not only in the center of the soul, but of society. This great white throne is set up among men because its roots are in the central society of the Godhead itself.

3. Being social, this moral authority must be historic. It is a rude view which regards society as contemporary alone. The living are but the latest; they are the fringe of society. We are but the outskirts of the race and inhabit the suburbs of time. The present is but the glowing tip of the past. For moral purposes and the affairs of the soul society includes the dead and their works, heaven, hell, and history. The longer the world lives, the more it is ruled by the dead. The majority of us are not with us. Our best wealth is chiefly legacy. I say nothing yet of the way in which we are ruled by the king of the unseen, the firstborn from the dead.

Moreover, the future lives and works in us. Posterity is a great factor in the present. Heredity has a retrospective action and comes up to us from the future as it descends on us from the past.

> There come up the stream
> Murmurs and scents of the infinite sea.

The conscience of the future determines our action today as well as the conscience of the past. The unborn deeply affect the generations that carry them; they affect our tastes, feelings, thought, and action. The present has the duties and emotions of a coming maternity. We were working in the men and movements of old. Parents obey their children in a subtle but real sense. There is in us an ethical presentiment and a spiritual providence, an entail from the anticipated, whereby we build better than we know. We own our solidarity with the future no less than our continuity with

the past, and we confess the beneficence to us of the posterity we bless.

It is not, therefore, in the midst of the present that the
seat of authority must be sought, but in the center of history,
of the soul. It is at the focus not of the age but of the race.
It is no more limited by the time than by the individual.
It is catholic for all time, never antiquated though ancient,
and as central at any one point of history as at another. Just
because it is central to history it is equally relevant to every
age, and the permanent contemporary of all time. If it
emerge at any point it is central to all.

4. The moral authority which is final must be not only
historic as a matter of fact but as a matter of essence and
principle. It must belong to the very nature and genius of
this authority that it be historic. It should not inhabit only
a remote world. It cannot rest in heaven; and it cannot
realize itself in the mystic depths of the individual; the
mystical is too individual to have authority. The true authority must press outward to take effect in events, in
action, in history. It is a self-bestowing, self-actualizing authority. The action of the race must not only give it an
area but an expression. It "finds itself" in history. It must
be authoritative for any age because it chiefly makes the
half-conscious age what it is. And so it must be not the past
alone, nor the future alone, but something which is the
same yesterday, today, and forever—the same not because
equally indifferent to past, present, and future, but because
equally fontal and creative—that is to say, it must be in its
nature revelation. The absolute power over us must be an
outgoing, self-giving power, translating itself into man; if
it mold the soul it must mold it to its own image. It descends on the soul, descends as a gift, as a self-bequest.

5. If the seat of authority be thus historic and not mystic,
social and not individual, ethical and not merely rational, it
must stand forth either as an institution or as a person in an

act. As a matter of fact it is between these that we are compelled to choose—between a church and a person. And history has written in the career of Catholicism the result of placing the ultimate ethical authority in the church as an institution. It is Jesuitism. The conscience of human society is not another society. The church is not the conscience of the state; nor is the conscience of the church the kingdom of God even. The kingdom itself is first constituted by the king; and the conscience of society is a personal holy will. Wherever the conscience of the conscience is an institution we lapse into some form of Machiavelianism or Jesuitry, according as the institution is state or church. No institution can be the conscience of the conscience without debasing it and in the end provoking a saving rebellion. If the conscience cannot be its own authority, it can at least be the death of every usurping authority. Only one Lord can sit this steed.

Conscience is not its own lord, but it is autonomous thus far, that its authority must be of its own nature—personal. It is heteronomous indeed; it demands an external authority. But it is an authority external to its range only and not to its nature. And an institution is foreign in its genius to the conscience; it is only a person that is akin. Only a soul can rule a soul, only a will redeem a captive will, only a living person be a source of grace. Holy and blessed as the church may be, it is but the channel of grace, and therefore only the organ and not the seat of authority.

6. But if the final authority be not an institution then it cannot be a canon, which is in the nature of an institution. It cannot be the Bible. The canon of Scripture was the work of the church, and if the church's work be final for the conscience then the church must be. The Bible is really a word of two meanings, with which we unconsciously juggle. It means the canon, and it means the gospel as the living soul of the canon; and the two things are not the same.

There is a great difference between the whole of the Bible and the Bible as a whole. The whole of the Bible is not authoritative, but the Bible as a whole is. The whole of the Bible is not authoritative, the soul of the Bible is. But even the Bible as a whole and soul is not, in strictness of thought, the *final* authority. The final authority is the gospel in the Bible, which is Jesus Christ and him as crucified. That is within the Bible; but it is to be got out (as I have said) not so much by dissection as by distillation. The gospel is not a dead portion of the Bible, but its living spirit. The testimony of Jesus is the spirit of all its prophecy.

The Bible broke the yoke of the church; but there are those to whom the Bible itself has become a yoke. They have forgotten that they were the Bible's sons and not its slaves. The gospel must do for the Bible what the Bible did for the church. The Bible has an authority that judges the church; and the gospel has an authority that judges the Bible. The gospel made the Bible, and the gospel must rule it. If the church had made the Bible, the church would rule it, and would be its final interpreter. If the Christian consciousness simply had made it, then it would still be at the mercy of the Christian consciousness. But it is not. Neither the church tradition nor the Christian consciousness is the final appeal. It is the gospel rather than the Bible, yea, rather than the character of Christ, that is the true last word of God. Christ himself was there for the sake of the gospel —for the work of grace and the word of redemption. The value of the Bible is not primarily for theology, but for redemption. It is there as an expression and witness of Christ in his saving work. The real solvent which is acting on the Bible at this moment is Christ and the power of his resurrection. It is the vast and growing action of Christ's redemption that is rending the gorgeous tomb and raising the lovely stone of Scripture, lest we should only embalm the Lord in his shrine. The Bible does not exist for the schools, but for the church, and especially for the practical function of the church with the world, its salvation. It is not there for sacred culture or sacred science, but for Christ and his one purpose of redemption. Its authority is due to its place and function in the service of the gospel. The final authority is the redeemer. The Bible is authoritative only in so far as it conveys and serves his redeeming work and purpose. It is regulative neither for science nor history, but for the soul. Its key and goal is the gospel, as God's forgiving act in Christ. And the varying value of each part is proportionate to its nearness and directness to this central aim. The touchstone of every book and passage is Christ, as Luther said; but it is Christ, not as the perfect character, but as the sole theme that Paul would know, Christ as the crucified redeemer. "Back to Christ" is a sound call; but it would mislead us if it meant merely back to his teaching as our norm and his character as our ideal. His teaching, as precept at least, does not cover all the moral ground, even where it is clear; and his character means for modern ears such a biography as we have not and never can have. Back to Christ means back to the gospel as it is in Christ, and especially in his atoning death. The supreme commentary on the Gospels is the gospel, as the key to Christ's life is his death.

We are free, nay, forced, therefore, to deal critically with all the parts of the Bible under the ruling principle of redemption. That principle prescribed both the power and the limitations of the redeemer himself; and it cannot but determine the scope and limits of the record. The critics may teach us to *place* each part; but we measure and weigh it by its contribution to that principle and end. Christ in the Bible judges the Bible, as the conscience in us judges us. The authority for the Bible is not the conscience, but that which is the authority for the conscience also. It is the redeemer of the conscience, who, through the redeemed conscience, sent forth the Bible to make just such claims upon men as the redemption that produced it—no less but no other. Both the Bible and church are products of the gospel, and they exercise what authority they have as servants of the gospel. And the servant is not above his Lord, nor even near his level. Both Bible and church may be the means of our faith but neither is the ground of our faith. If Protestantism have any meaning it is that the ground of our faith is identical with the object of our faith—which is God reconciling the world in the cross of Christ. The Reformation was not the rediscovery of the Bible chiefly, but of the gospel in the Bible. And it stood not for the supremacy of conscience, but for the rescue of the conscience by the supremacy of Christ in it. And of Christ in it, not as the supreme rabbi to solve cases, but as the author and principle of a new life and spirit which solves cases age after age by an indwelling grace, and truth, and love, and light, and power.

7. My drift has already escaped. There is but one authority which corresponds to all the conditions I have named, that is ethical, social, historic, personal, living and present. It is revealed, absolutely given, and for ever miraculous to human thought as the divine forgiveness always must be. It is the grace of God to us sinners in the cross of Christ that is the final moral authority as being the supreme nature and act of the supreme moral being. And it is for ever a wonder to human thought except in so far as it has made in man its own thought. It is not irrational, it is rational; but it is not in reason to realize its own deep nature and content till it is redeemed. And the redemption of Christ not only satisfies the natural conscience which is its herald, but it opens to it a new world even within itself. The thoughts of many hearts are revealed as well as the purpose of God. It provides a new standard and ideal which it guarantees as the final reality and *therefore* the final authority. It re-

veals in the conscience new needs, and raises it to appreciate the moral value and right of a doctrine like atonement, which to its mere light of nature seemed strange and incredible.

The grace of God to the conscience in the historic but perennial cross of Christ must be the one source of morals and the final seat of authority to a race that is redeemed or nothing—redeemed or lost. Natural and theological ethics may be separated for convenience of academic discussion; but in the final experience of the race there is no ethic but a theological. All morals are but academic which fail to recognize that the greatest fact in social ethics is also the most formidable and intractable. It is the fact of sin and guilt. We must take man in his actual historic situation; and if we do this the so-called natural conscience does not exist. It is an abstraction; and what exists is the historic product, the sinful conscience. So much as that solidarity and heredity may teach us. If, then, we so take man, whoever masters that fact of sin is master, effective and sole master, of the conscience, and so of the whole of human life, of history and of society. The redeemer from moral death is the seat of authority for all mankind, in their affairs as in their faith. For practical purposes, on the collective human scale, on the scale of the whole passionate, actual soul, we must deal with the evangelical conscience, shaped by faith in the redeemer, when we ask for the seat of final authority for the race. The ethics of the future must be the explication of the cross—and of the cross understood as a gospel and not as an ideal, as an atonement and not as a classic sacrifice.

8. I would present the matter, in fine, from this point of view, and indicate how it is only a deep and expiatory view of atonement that invests Christ with this final moral claim, or the cross with its ultimate authority.

The whole race is not only weighted with arrears but infected with a blight. The train of history is not simply late, but there has been an accident, and an accident due to malice and crime. We struggle not only with misfortune but with a curse. The total and ultimate moral situation of the race is not moral only but religious. It is a spiritual and not only an ethical crisis. The malady and the remedy are religious both. The Lord and master of the race is not merely "a self-transcending goodness," even if we regard that goodness as personal and ideal. He is a redeemer. He not only *embodies* goodness, and startles us with the wonder and love of our ideal selves, but he *intervenes* with his goodness as the only condition of our release, and of our power to fulfill ourselves and share his life. My king and Lord is not only my helper, but he who gives me back the life I had thrown away and lost the power to regain. My sovereign deigns to contend with rebel me, and, when he has disarmed me, gives me back my sword and takes me into his service. And he is especially and absolutely king and Lord when we realize *how* he became redeemer, what is the nature of the moral act by which he saved the spiritual situation of the race. His authority does not rest simply on our grateful sense of his kindness. It is not alone that we are melted and mastered by the spectacle of his tender mercy and his love that will not let us go. It has a more objective ground. That is too subjective and unstable for a seat of authority universal and spiritual, absolute and eternal. Nor does it rest on our admiring sense of his goodness. It is not that he produces on us the impression of one who incarnates excellence, concentrates human worth, anticipates in himself the moral future of humanity, and sets it forth as an ideal to man and a surety to God. All that is fine, but for the purposes of the conscience and its absolute authority it is too aesthetic. He remains still outside the living center, conflict, and tragedy of the will. The seat of his absolute authority is neither in our wonder, fascination, nor gratitude. He is not king because he personalizes the divine life. Nor is he our master because he incarnates the holy law; for that would be but condensing in a personality the very power our sin had most reason to dread. *Holiness* becomes even more terrible in the holy *one*. But he redeemed us from the curse of the law being made a curse for us. He satisfied for us that holy law which our sin could break but never unseat, whose wounded claim no future obedience or even penitence of ours could ever extinguish, which at once lifts us from the dust and grinds us to powder, which it is our dignity to touch and our misery to remember, on which the most titanic human defiance dashes in vain, and which masters our loudest freedom with a quiet inextinguishable irony and a slow inevitable judgment. That was our absolute master as Christ found us. And that was the judgment that he absorbed in his holy love. By extinguishing through loving sacrifice the claims of this law he became their reversionary over us. Our high priest became our final judge. He took over in his person the lien held on our sinful conscience by all the moral order of the world and all the holy righteousness of God. He acquired the claim he extinguished. He became our moral world, our spiritual realm. By his complete obedience to God's holy law he is identified with it in its immovable right over us, and so he becomes in himself and his redeeming act the moral master of the race. Because he took man's judgment he became man's judge. Because he exhausted the curse he acquired the monopoly of blessing. He who met the whole law became the law's Lord. And the Lord of the law of the conscience is for conscience its king. He is the conscience of the conscience because he is the redeeming conscience of Holy God. He is thus the fountain of moral honor and the center of spiritual authority for ever. He would be supreme indeed if our orderly moral nature were only constituted in him; but he is absolutely and forever supreme because our disordered nature is in him redeemed. And the moral authority of society has at the long last only an evangelical base.

A true and deep evangelicalism, therefore, is not a party in the church, but it is the very being of the church. The coming church must be an evangelical church. While she has this note the church has the secret of the social future. Everything turns on the cross and the nature of the cross's grace. Is the spiritual power of society the moral mastery of Christ's cross? There is no question in the world so vital to society as this of the spiritual power. The temperance question, the sexual question, the war question, the Irish question, the Negro question, the question of labor, the question of the proletariat, and other such are most grave and pressing. But none of them are so grave and deep, in the long run, as the question of the spiritual power. Society coheres with many abuses, but it cannot remain society without a spiritual power. What shall that be, and where is its seat? It is really the church question. No question of philanthropy, however urgent and moving we feel it, has the importance of this. For it has the future and permanence of philanthropy itself within it. It is possible to vulgarize any question, and more easy the greater, finer, and subtler it is. And the church question is much vulgarized. The no-popery cry can be vulgar enough. But the issue is great and spiritual enough to outlive all that. It will be always with us, and always nearer. It is not extinct, it is only in abeyance. It retires for a longer leap. That the Christian question is a social question is now a truism in theory, though it is not yet a commonplace of practice. But that does not mean that it passes from the churches to the politicians, economists, and socialists. It means rather that by the will of Christ the Christian problem cannot be solved except by a Christian society —by a church. And it means that we must be more concerned to choose between the various churches, especially between the two great Western churches, the Catholic and the Protestant, the theurgic and the evangelical, the magical and the moral; for with one of them the social future lies, social authority and social safety; and it does not lie with the other. What lies with the other is social collapse. We must work in a church. Mere individual efforts at social reform, if they are very radical, are but quixotic, and break fruitless and miserable on the entrenchments of wrong. To change the world convert the church. It is through a society that the Savior wills to save society, and when we make our choice we have but to ask which church gives effect to the New Testament cross, to the moral authority of the spiritual cross. Which is built on the gospel as I have explained it —as an act and a power, rather than a creed? Which has that authority? Which, therefore, has the divine commission? Is it the church whose secret is in its organization or in its gospel, which is institutional or moral, which is graceful in its sacraments or sacramental in its grace, whose word asks for mere assent or for the obedience of faith, whose authority has its seat on a venerable spot of earth or utters its still more venerable and awful voice seated in the center of the redeemed conscience? We must have for these days an authority which is *in its nature* emancipatory and not repressive, empowering and not enfeebling. That authority is the redeemer's. The object of human faith must be the source of human freedom, individual or social. Society can only be saved by what saves the soul. The evangelical contention is that that object of faith is the redeemer, directly and alone. It is the straitness of the cross that is the condition of critical, speculative, and social freedom for the world. The church of the future is the church of one article, which has the simplicity of a whole and the greatness of the soul. And the concentration of the evangelical churches upon that infinite and creative point of redemption alone is the one answer by which Protestantism can meet a claim so bold, thorough, and commanding as the dogma of papal infallibility. Mere Catholicism is powerless against Vaticanism, which is Catholicism made perfect.

Our gospel is not the property of a religious group however large, or of a religious organization however hoary. But it is the one public power, the one person, by which human society is saved, not only for God but for itself. It is society that is being saved, and not only a group of individuals, an elect out of society. And the one saving power is the living Word and gospel of Jesus Christ the crucified, risen, and royal redeemer, who is over all and blessed forevermore.

8.   The Soul of Christ and the Cross of Christ

Forsyth underscored the gospel of grace in preaching. In a prior work he urged the preacher not to attempt "to heal the hurt of God's people lightly." In *This Life and the Next,* Forsyth defines that grace as holy love which is grace to the sinner. "It is what love brings or grace gives. Only holy can love forever; only holy can completely forgive." In a quite lyrical passage Forsyth returns to this theme of holiness.

> The reversion of the world will belong to that church which makes most of the holiness of God, with its outgoing as love, and its downgoing as grace. The world will belong to the church which takes most seriously the mercy which is rooted there. 'As is thy majesty, so is thy mercy.' What a phrase! What an inspiration! To be in the Apocrypha too, outside the pale of reputable inspiration.[1]

This basic theme of the cross Forsyth set forth in his remarkable sermon of 1896 entitled, "God the Holy Father." There the evangelical theology of Peter Taylor Forsyth rings a clarion call or is it a tocsin to the entire 20th century church. Written as it was while Forsyth was in Cambridge,

---

[1]*London Quarterly Review* CXVI(1911), p. 209.

it deserves a fresh hearing in the English churches of 1970.
Theology "is a matter of grace meeting sin by sacrifice to
holiness, more even than of love meeting need by service to
man." [2] Unless such a serious note is heeded, "a faith merely
experimental becomes merely empirical, and at last dies
of secularity." [3]

* * *

From the *London Quarterly Review*
CXVI (October, 1911)

I.

Impression and Confession

One reason why the church does not impress the world
more may be because we are too much bent on impressing
it, more bent on impressing than on confessing. We labor
on the world rather than overflow on it. We have a deeper
sense of its need than of our own fullness, of its problems
than of our answer. We do more to convey salvation to
others than to cultivate it in ourselves, to save than to
testify. We are tempted to forget that we have not, in the
first place, either to impress the world or to save it, but
heartily and mightily to confess in word and deed a Savior
who has done both, who has done it for ourselves, and who
is doing it every day. A man's *inspiration* impresses an
audience, but it is his *revelation* only which recreates the
world. If the blood of the martyrs was the seed of the
church it was because their fidelity was a witness and an
offering presented to Christ rather than to the world, and
the more impressive as it did not seek to impress, but only
to be true. The kind of religion that carries *us* through the
world will say more than all *our* efforts to carry *it* into the
world. Sanctity tells more than energy at last, since it

[2]*God the Holy Father,* p. 5.
[3]"The Place of Spiritual Experience in the Making of Theology," preached
at Birmingham in 1906. Quoted in J. K. Mozley, *The Heart of the Gospel,*
p. 76.

produces the only energy that at last does tell. Nothing but a holy church can sanctify the world; and a holy church means a church of the holy Word and the souls it new creates. A missionary church must in its heart be more of a worshiping church than a working church. In either case it is a confessing church first of all. It can only live *for* Christ to Christian purpose if it live *in* him so that he live through it. Any true efficiency for Christ flows at last from proficiency of soul. For religious effect is one thing and spiritual efficiency is another. And the danger of the religious public is to take the one for the other, and to pursue effect impatiently with other means than efficiency.

The great Missionary Conference in Edinburgh in June, 1910, is not the only sign that we are in the midst of a missionary age of the church. Let us not identify the whole *extensive* aspect of the church's action on the world with foreign missions. And we shall not, if we consider the immense interest and energy of the church, for the last half-century at least, in connection with philanthropy in the voluntary field, and with social reform in the political program.

But for the moment I am not thinking of either home or foreign missions in the ordinary sense. What impresses one as the most missionary feature of the church of the present is neither of these things by themselves, but the whole temper and direction of the church's mind. It is centrifugal. It works outwards. It thinks imperially. The whole quality of its religion is marked by a ruling interest in the aspects of Christianity which appeal to those outside the church rather than to those within, whether in the evangelical, social, or apologetic way. And therewithal it does not feel equal to the task it owns, or the ideal it pursues. Its ideal is greater than its power.

We hear complaints which may or may not be true about the poverty of preaching. The more experienced Christians

especially complain that in much of the preaching of the day
they find little to feed the riper needs of the believing soul.
They note the taste for quite young men as preachers, men
who will get at the young or the outsider, but who cannot
yet have the word for the old disciples. They mark the
welcome which churches give to various forms of work that
bear upon the religious world rather than upon the faithful
church itself. They note, for instance, that the study of
the child is more interesting to many in the church than the
study of the Bible, and a boys' brigade will often get more
attention than a Bible class. They perceive the keen interest of the preacher in the points where Christian faith
touches philosophy, science, politics, or civics. They mark
his prevalently apologetic sympathies, or his zeal for the
humanism in Christianity, for a natural religion highly
spiritualized, and his comparative lack of interest in the
great themes of positive revelation, such as the Trinity, or
in the distinctive theology of faith which gathers about a
matter like justification. He preaches about subliminal psychology (they say), and even founds theology on it; but he
is less at home in matters like regeneration, and such things
as involve the moral psychology of the specific Christian experiences rather than touch the marches of the church and
the world. He is more familiar with the reformer's perpetual
energy than the saint's everlasting rest.

And these observers, critics, and complainants are not
wholly wrong. The problem handled everywhere is how to
reach people rather than how to teach them. The eye of
the church is directed outward rather than inward, to
ingathering rather than upbuilding. I speak broadly, but
it seems to me that we are more preoccupied with the compass than with the content of the gospel. We scheme how
to cover and capture the world's mind rather than to develop
that of the church; how to commend Christ to those who
are not Christian than how to enrich him for those that

are; how to extend the area of faith than how to improve its estate, like an absentee landlord who is wild for the empire.

All such features mean the predominance of the extensive side of Christianity. And there are signs that this overbalance to the missionary side endangers its own end. The extensive action of Christianity grows slack because it outruns its base in the church's intensive growth. "We cannot send reinforcements because we do not make recruits," said Dr. Denney at Edinburgh. There are many grounds for suspecting that the real and intractable reasons for the decay in certain churches of interest in foreign missions are such as these—the impoverishment of faith's working capital in their own experience, the thinness of their Christianity as an inmost life, the lack in their religion of that note of 'intimacy' which is such a feature of modern literature, or of the positivity and thoroughness that go with modern science, and the poverty of mass, and volume, and driving power behind their contact with the world. It is a loss which robs their impact of much force, and therefore much result that it would otherwise have.

There is an historical reason for this sense of impotence on the church's part. The idea of humanity which has taken possession of the age has not grown out of the church's faith so much as it has been infused into it. It arose outside the church, in that great modern departure which began with Lessing and went on through Rousseau, to take command of our time. It is only in a secondary sense a Christian idea. It is not without some violence that we find it in the New Testament. Here the prime idea is the kingdom of God, or the new humanity, the new creation, to which the natural race is secondary and contributory—a soil for the seed. What rules in Christianity is the idea of the new humanity created in Jesus Christ, not the natural humanity glorified. The destiny of the race is Christ and his kingdom, as the gift of God, not the mere exaltation of civilization as a human product. But at the end of the eighteenth century the conception of Christian faith had fallen low. The Reformation theology had settled on its lees. The evangelical movement, great as it was, had not the universal note, except partially in its missions. It had not the public note. And upon a church thus starved and straitened in its own resources there broke the modern humanist enthusiasm. It was received with joy and ardor by multitudes whose higher sympathy and imagination found nothing large enough in the sects and orthodoxies which dominated the church. And while it carried many out of the church, it made a new inspiration to many also who remained within. Their Christian faith seemed to offer many points of attachment to the new ideal, which rather infected it from without than inspired it from within. This is an inversion of the true Christian order, which must always find in humanity points of attachment for faith, and not in faith points of attachment for humanity. Moreover, the idea of humanity remains an idea till it find in the faith of the new humanity in Christ the power to give it practical effect. It is a great and divine idea, and the mind of the church must be tuned to it. But even yet we only dump it on the old creed; we do not join them up. For that time, the actual faith of the church was certainly below the range and flight of the humane ideal. And not even yet has it undergone a development commensurate with the sympathy or imagination of the new passion. The rank and file of the church have been facing the enthusiasm of humanity with a theology and a religion which were but individualist, sectarian, or nationalist at most. Now these particularist forms of Christian faith are passing. Both theology and faith are undergoing a great change at the hands, especially, of the cautious representatives of a renovated theology. These things are, and should be, slower to change than either ideals, sympathies, or imaginations. But the church is slowly realizing the trust committed to it of a truly racial Christ and his salvation. At the same time it is protesting against the humanist transfer of the Christian center of gravity from God to man. But the happy change has not yet reached the masses of the church as the humanitarian idea has done. And as a result they do not find in their type of faith the resources adequate to the call upon them to cover and command and bless the world. They are torn with the attempt to work the idea of humanity with a faith whose note is still too individual, too sectarian, too national, and too narrow. The impression they strive to create is wider than the confession they are able to make.

We are all familiar, and to a certain extent sympathetic, with one way suggested to improve our effect on outsiders. It is the method of what some would call reduction, some concentration in the matter of belief. It bids us drop much of our inherited message, and shut down upon what is common to us with other faiths, or with the world at its best. It says we are carrying to those without and afar a lumber of thought which is more of the West than of the East, or more of the evangelical than of the spiritual, more of the temporary than of the eternal. It even impresses on us that evangelical Christianity is but one form of it, that because some men need forgiving grace all do not, and that this form can be dropped to much advantage in certain circumstances where we confront a greater or less measure of culture, whether at home or abroad. It presses the fallacy that Christ is more than the gospel, and that we should concentrate on him either as a symbol or a person, and avoid the theological corollaries which are associated with his work of redemption in the cross. This is impressed upon us sometimes in unpleasant forms, which, however, are only the performance of a striking tune on a street organ. Men who by their weight, knowledge, and piety deserve respect and attention can charm us much more wisely with the same strain. And they make some to see—what others had realized on no compulsion save that of an ever-deepening faith and its liberty—that we were much straitened in the old armour, and that we can march, maneuver, and fight better as peltasts than as hoplites of belief.

The religious public is much relieved to recognize this reduction in the Christian's marching weight. And it is slaying the slain to insist on it. Where guidance is really wanted is with a problem beyond the liberalism that trades in platitudinarian generalities of this kind, a problem which buckles us down to ask just where the line is to be drawn which divides reduction from collapse. The proverbial old man was within sight of getting his ass down to living on a straw a day when unluckily it died. What is it that we are really to carry to the world—a pure gift and new creation from God, or some brotherly aid to help the weak and trust the best in us all? When Christ's word is in collision with the modern consciousness at its best, are we to be reduced so far as to say that it is Christ that must go? Is our liberal and portable gospel a fatherhood which is obtained by deflating Christianity of its Christology and packing it in an attractive cover? If not, if we have a real and positive gift from God, what precisely is it? Is it the soul of Christ, or the work of Christ, the mystic soul or the moral work? Is it the inner life, the moral power and spiritual impressiveness, of the historic Christ who is also the living heavenly Christ, or the cross of Christ as the marrow and point of both for our justification? Granted that Christianity is a matter of experience, what is it that the ripe Christian experiences—a mighty ideal presence, or a Savior once for all? Who and what is the living Christ? Is it the interior personality, of which the cross was but an incidental by-product, or is it the Christ whose inaccessible inmost life ran up into the cross, was condensed, and pointed for our justification on the cross, and only by the cross made intelligible at all? Is the cross, as Herrmann says, more valuable for the theological reflection of the few than for the faith's foundation of all? And is our living Christ what he says—one to whom only the collective church has access and not the single soul?

Behind all the creaking or breaking of the missionary machinery the real trouble of missions is in the region of the inspiring faith, and such of its problems as I have named. And it lies not so much in the absence of faith, but in the abeyance (as the church's note) of the kind of faith that created the church, spread it, and alone can spread it still.

Now there is no doubt that our preoccupation with the impact of Christ on the surface of the outside world rather than with his action in the depths of the believer's soul disposes us to concentrate on his powerful and mysterious personality (and often only on his character), and to ignore what I have ventured to call elsewhere the cruciality of his cross, which is such a scandal to the world. Paul also seems to have had to do with some Christians who were Christ's men but enemies of the cross of Christ. We are invited to think that the most valuable thing in Christianity is not that which appeals to the ripe Christian or the great penitents, but that which attracts those who are not ill-disposed but aloof. We are tempted, as we dwell on the personality of Christ, to treat him as a deep mystery to be revered rather than a clear revelation to be trusted, as our new Moses rather than our new creator. He winningly impresses on a subjective age the abysmal depths of a divine personality more than he effects in the waiters for salvation the eternal reality and world-purpose of God. But which is the central and final function of Christ?

Does Christianity rest at last on that sympathetic or imaginative side which most commends it to non-believers, to the most religious or most needy side of the world? Or does it rest on that spiritual and eternal redemption which

gives it its power for the veteran confessors and the mighty
experients who have become the classics of the faith and
the church? Granting that many today are moved by the
figure of Christ, by the picture stepping out of its scriptural
frame on them, can they stop there? Can such an impression carry the weight of life and conscience to the end?
Herrmann's *Verkehr*, for instance, is a great illuminative,
spiritual, and almost devotional book, but could his position
carry a church? Can it surmount the ravages of criticism,
and carry certainty through the worst that the world may
do and our own weakness dread? Is that impression the
real foundation of a new and eternal relation to God? It
may be its *Erkentnissgrund,* is it its *Realgrund?* It may
arrest and even subdue us, could it regenerate and establish
us forever? I have never felt convinced myself by those
passages in which he seeks to show how his position leaves
him immune from the worst that criticism can inflict.

It is a very important question, this, and one that leads
us very far. Is the Godhead of Jesus best expressed, and
best founded for us, in that humane godliness of his which
must affect all decent people, or in that God-forsakenness of
his which has meant so much for both the reprobate and
the saint? It is a question which breaks up into several
forms. Let us admit, provisionally, that the door into faith
is one thing; the ground, when we are well within, another;
and the rich content and plerophory of it, when we are
'far ben,' and settled in, is still a third. Let us keep distinct
the rise of faith, the rock of faith, and its range; its font, its
foundation, and its fullness; what produces it in the be-
ginner, what supports it in experience, what expands it, in
the ripe, to a scheme of the eternal world.

What then, we ask, is the relation between these phases?

When we are occupied with what initiates and begets
faith we have the church's extensive or missionary interest,
the father church; when we are engaged with what supports

it, or is its foundation, we have the church's intensive, worshiping, edifying, or nursing interest, the cherishing church, the mother church; and when we are concerned with the rich range and fullness of faith we have the church's distensive interest, its self exposition or evolution, its theological interest, the cosmic church. We have the gracious church, the holy church, and the glorious church of the gracious, holy, glorious God. How, then, we ask, are these related? Are we to say, for instance, that in appealing to the weak or the world we must use the fascination of the character of Christ; while in address to the mature Christian we must use the real ground of faith's confidence with God—Christ's work concentrated in the cross; and only then, when we come to speak wisdom among the perfect, must we dwell on the fullness of faith as it is expressed in the Godhead of Christ or the holiness of the Trinity? To the young shall we offer Christ's sympathetic charm, to the ripe his moral realism, to the mellow his spiritual range?

The question grows more acute if we reduce the issues from three to two. Granting, for the moment, that we should go to those we want to win with the inner life and spell of Christ, is that to be the staple still of our address to those who are won, who are truly within the church? And, whereas we used to refer these last to the foundation of faith, namely the cross, shall we now erase the second distinction, and relegate that work of the cross to the third division (now the second) which contains the implified thought of faith or its speculative theology? Shall we keep both the catechumens and the members upon the inner life of Christ and the impressions it makes on us, finding there both the origin of faith and its ground; and shall we dismiss the work of Christ from our direct religion to the theological schools, and class it among the luxuries of faith? Shall we say that faith is primarily concerned with impression from Christ both for the young and the old, and only secondarily with justification, which is for the divines and the schools? Shall we abolish the distinction between the order of time and the order of value, between the first founding of faith and its abiding foundation; and, whereas we used to say that the soul of Christ came first in the way of time, as faith's introduction, while the work of Christ was prime through all, as faith's ground, shall we now say that the soul of Christ is both prior and prime, at once our first step and our final footing, and that the effect of Christ's work is otiose, and left to the speculation and leisure of those whose taste lies that way?

To do that is to alter the whole message of the church. And to displace thus the cross of Christ is also to truncate his soul. It sacrifices to the inner Christ the inmost and the holiest of all.

II.

Pushing the Gospel and Preaching It

There is no doubt, I think, that the extensive or missionary side has so far got the upper hand in the church that its ruling and favorite interest is in what makes the gospel welcome to the young, the weak, or the world; that we are more concerned about getting people into a wide and easy church, with a facile manhood, than about getting them deep into a humbling, taxing, and sifting Christ, with a manhood proved and braced; that we are more occupied, and more successful, in extending the social pale of Christ than in establishing his profound power; that the extensive aspect gets the better of the intensive, the quantitative of the qualitative, or, as one might say, the crops of the mines; and that the disciplinary apparatus of the intensive action of a holy gospel is being scrapped on the heap where the distensive results of faith already lie discredited, like a doctrine of the Trinity, as mere theology.

And what is the result? The church grows too missionary

for its success. It grows too exclusively missionary even for missions. It grows more cosmopolite than missionary, more ecumenical than truly catholic. It tends to occupy more territory than it can hold. Religion is running out of the church as action upon the world more rapidly than it is running into it as action on the soul; and as its level sinks, and its volume shrinks, it weight and pressure on life is reduced. Work preoccupies us till we lose the faith that carries it on, and the business of the kingdom suffers from the very busyness of its sons. As we are busy here and there the spirit is gone. We totally misinterpret the passage about doing the will of God as a means of knowing the doctrine. There is no promise there that practical Christianity is the organ of access to Christian truth. That is putting the cart before the horse. We need certainty of Christian truth for true and sustained Christian action. And all that the well-worn passage said was that those who had inner obedience to God for a life habit would know, by a spiritual free-masonry, when they heard Christ teaching, that he was religiously neither an adventurer nor a self-seeker, but the vehicle of a real inspiration, whether its theological form was perfect and final or not. They would know that he was inspired enough to say with divine authority that no amount of practical obedience of the conscientious kind, were it as careful as that of the elder brother, could win to know the truth of a God of grace apart from the obedience of the prodigal which is faith and repentance. The last truth about God can be reached by neither thought nor duty, but by tasting the grace of God. And as a matter of fact history has often shown that men of loose life may hold the most true and exalted doctrines about life and God; while on the other hand, men of severe and devoted life may hold doctrines too stiff and hard to have come from the God and Father of Jesus Christ. At the present day we may often find that the very best of practical Christians have an utterly impossible theology, and that both the believer and the unbeliever can often be very wrong whose life seems completely right.

Every missionary society complains of the starving of missions; and the source of it, paradoxical as it may seem, is really missionary hyperthrophy. "A lamp's death when, o'er-fed with oil, it chokes." We are so engrossed with the pushing, adventurous, attractive, winning, or impressive side of Christianity that we neglect by comparison the real searching evangelical core which guarantees the going power. A preacher who can fill a church will not be much criticized in respect of his message; and a genial or kindly personality will atone for much treason to faith. We compass sea and land with a gospel whose action on ourselves at home is so ineffectual that foreign converts could not be trusted to visit the land that converted them. Our imperial policy outgrows our home resources of personal faith and sacrifice. We gain the world, but we lose in soul. We pursue a simple and welcome faith, but we lose a holy and judging faith. We cover the earth, but our note is not unearthly. Men admire our energy more than they wonder at our spell. To substitute a soul of Christ which submerges his work for the work of Christ which effectuates his soul is to cultivate an inverted faith, and one more likely to increase the church than to strengthen it, to popularize it for a time than to sanctify it in the eternal spirit. To find the central and effective revelation of God in the impression produced by Christ's inner life rather than in the redemption by his inmost death is to miss the revelation that the conscience most needs. It is to evangelize the whole world from a center but partly evangelized, which itself needs the extension of the gospel into its dark places. What needs God's revelation is the conscience, more even than the heart or the spiritual nature. There is no sweeter word than God's lovingkindness, but it is not so holy as his judgment on him who was made sin for our righteousness. When we put the matter on a world scale the supreme problem is a question of having the conscience forgiven rather than of having the heart filled. And even for the conscience it is not a question of theology, of believing in God's power and will to deal with human sin; it is a question of private religion, of finding him dealing with my personal guilt. Truly it is much to realize that Christ is God's answer to the moral anomalies and wrongs of life. It is still more to see him as God's reaction upon the sin of the world. But it is most of all to be sure that he destroys my personal guilt which burdens, blackens, and curses all. No mere impression from the soul of Christ can destroy that, only God in Christ crucified as the justifier of the ungodly. Only the cross of Christ can do it, as the supreme work of God, and the supreme reaction of the holy one upon an evil world. It can only be done by a revelation which is in its nature redemption, by a revelation which is not merely redemptive in its tendency and destiny, but which is already a finished salvation. We need something beyond the certainty that God in Christ *will at last be* more than a match for sin; we need the certainty that he *has been* the death of our guilt. And there is no such certainty but in an atoning Christ as crucified and risen. A sense of the pressure of personal guilt is a better qualification for understanding the cross than even the sense of the world's sin. To say "rivers of water run down mine eyes, because they keep not thy law," does not bring us so near to the God whose sacrifices are a broken and contrite spirit as the confession "mine iniquities have taken hold of me, so that I cannot look up." It is a great thing to say amidst misunderstanding and neglect, "my judgment is *with* my God," but it is a far greater and more solemn thing for the aching conscience to say "my judgment is *upon* my God." And if we feel that to speak like this may look like the pharisaism of the publican, that it suggests something so hateful as turning our defect into a quality, making an advantage out of our shame, and drawing from it a certain eminence, then we turn from ourselves altogether to take refuge in the history of the church's central, classic, and evangelical experience. It is the church's penitence that has given it its best conscience and its best insight into its Savior. And it testifies that neither the revelation of Christ's inner life, nor even its entrance into us as a mere infused spirit, can give us the last peace when once the specter of our personal guilt has begun to walk. It is not enough that his presence should tread and calm the raging waters of our remorse. He is there not simply to fulfill our spiritual aspirations, to increase our moral power, or to relieve us from the burden and pressure of an untoward world. His redemption is deeper and higher than all that. It goes to the depths of our conscience—from the holy heights of God. God is in him reconciling, atoning, and not imputing. We must have a holy act of God as real as any act which made our guilt, and as final. For if God's saving act is not final our damning act is.

Moreover, for the church to found and fasten its faith, not upon what commends Christ to the ripe Christian conscience, but upon what sounds most worthy, humane, and welcome in him outside the church, is suicide. Does Christianity, for instance, really stand or fall by its success in winning the vote for Christ of the working class, by leading them to rise up at his coming while they kneel down to none, not even to him? The church does not stand or fall by its relation to the outside world, or its action on it, but by its relation and commerce with God. If that be right, free, and full, our action on the world will not fail at last, either in ethic, conversion, or benevolence. The nemesis of the external standard is seen, first, in this, that it does not really secure the respect even of the world—as no man does who deprecates or neglects his own individuality in the effort to be agreeable. After all we are justified by our faith, even to the world. And, second, the nemesis is seen in the way in which a belief in Christ, reduced from his cross to his inner soul, tends to ebb down to the denial of his historic existence for the sake of his idea. It tends thus to ebb as soon as we lose hold of the one thing in him which is the substance of history—a great soul not simply contemplated or revered (which is aesthetic religion), but put wholly into a great and decisive act. Cast loose from the cross, from redemption as the focus of revelation, we reach at the long last the conviction that:

> . . . the ray that led us on
> Shines from a long annhilated star.

A constant weakness of the church as catholic is the peril of that ambition to the church as holy. The missionary passion to spread may outrun the sanctified passion to grow. The effort to subdue the world may starve all effort to master the word, and the world is apt to be gained at the cost of the church's soul. The church as messenger may starve the church as mother; and she may fall to the position of those public persons who lose character in pressing a cause, and cease to be good in the passion to be apostles and martyrs. This we recognize in the history and fall of Roman Catholicism, where the empire church submerges the gospel church, and the curia of cardinals crushes the communion of saints. But the like peril might subtly await other churches in proportion as they are imperial and aggressive. They might be zealous for missions and yet treat the grand idea of mother church as only suggesting something romish. The free churches run no risk from Catholicism in the popular sense of the word. They are safe from the priest, and the mass, and the pope. But they are not safe from the dream of Catholicism, the passion to cover the world at home or abroad with Christianity, or to compass sea and land with the church, by other means than the native power of a positive and experienced gospel in sacramental men. We are not safe from the peril of getting men in faster than the gospel can go, and winning more subjects for Christ than he can. Jesus, for all his love of souls, and for all his revelation of a Father who seeketh men to worship him, did not force himself on men. It is as true to say he eluded them. He did not assert his power over men by an obvious, an obtrusive, pursuit of them. We are in our own way liable to the peril of being catholic at the cost of sanctity, and cultivating a wide church or a broad church, at the cost of a holy church, deep and high. We too run the risk that befell ancient Rome and its modern Christian avatar in Romanism—the risk of being drained of liberty and strength at home by foreign conquest, the risk of acquiring a multitude of souls that we can neither manage nor inspire, that weight us more than steady us. The heart may lose power to sustain the energy of the limbs. We, too, as churches may lose the note of holiness, and the theology of the holy, in our own spiritual way. But is it not certain that a missionary church can only flourish as a mother church? The strength of the gathering church is the cherishing church. It can only spread from a warm and holy home. If we do not tend the altar lamps and the sacred hearth in church life, we profit the kingdom little in Christian work. And we can remain both universal and spiritual, the church can be at once catholic and holy, only on the condition of being also, and first, apostolic, i.e. of living on the depth and authority of the apostolic gospel. The church of a personal enthusiasm even for Christ will do no more for the world than Roman institutionalism unless it can transcend an enthusiasm of humanity which has Christ merely for its minister; unless it is, in the depth of its experienced conviction, an evangelical church, upon the foundation of redemptive fact and the faith and passion of reconciling holiness. For religious enthusiasm, as such, is no more a guarantee of the Holy Ghost than is canonical ordination.

The reversion of the world will belong to that church which makes most of the holiness of God, with its outgoing as love, and its downgoing as grace. The world will belong to the church which takes most seriously the mercy which is rooted there. "As is thy majesty, so is thy mercy." What a phrase! What an inspiration! To be in the Apocrypha too, outside the pale of reputable inspiration! There is no such mightly miracle anywhere as the union of God's most holy majesty and his most intimate mercy. One thing is stronger than the pity of the strong, and it is the pity of the holy. And it exists for us only in the cross of Christ. It is the incredible word of the cross, the very matter and marrow of Christianity, the moral lever to lift the world.

What is indicated therefore is not that the manner of gospel which is most engaging and welcome to the world should necessarily give the type for the church, but that what God has given us as the type for the church should go to the world in the most engaging and welcome way. That is to say, the mature church should not be confined to live on the inner life of Christ, nor on the inner life and subjective "holiness" of its own members, at the cost of Christ's inmost work on the cross as faith's real and certain ground; but the cross should be presented to the world (insinuated if you will) with that end foremost, so to say. It was for the objective work of the cross that the whole inner life of Christ was there. True, it was by the life of Christ that he began to act upon the disciples in their call. But that life itself was the retroaction of the cross. It was the cross that gathered it all up, showed what the purpose and principle of the life was, and made it effectual and decisive for the spiritual and eternal world. The cross certainly walked in on men, so to speak; it walked into men's hearts by a dear intimacy, it did not drop out of the sky. But it was the cross that walked in. The soul of Christ had the cross in its principle; the cross of Christ was his soul in power. It cannot be that what stirs faith at first should be really a different thing from the object of faith at last; and the object of faith is not only Christ but Christ consummate, Christ as crucified and risen. Is it not best after all to go to aliens with what we can heartily say is most precious and powerful to ourselves? Shall we ever exert true missionary power, speak with winning authority, and turn the world, unless we go (as wisely as may be) with the object of our faith as also the access to our faith: with the soul of a Christ who lived for the cross even when he hoped and prayed the cross might pass; and not with a Christ who lived wondrously winsomely, impressively, and just met with the cross? A faith produced by impressions from Christ's soul sinks in sand unless it come upon the rock of Christ's cross. Impressionist religion is not faith. And impressions, even from Christ, will not carry faith, though they may be made to grow to it.

But the real answer to our question is the answer to another. Where has God placed the true foundation of faith? Is it in Christ's soul or in his cross? If we take the whole New Testament Christ, he has placed it less directly in the historic fact of the person than in the apostolic Word of the cross. The last Christian fact is the total Word of the gospel in Christ, personal, crucified, and risen; it is not a powerful historic personality. It is not the epiphany of a person, but the purpose and work that crystallized it. The gospel is more theological than even biographical. Is that not clear from the history of the disciples' own faith? Truly they were educated through stages, and ripened by degrees. The impression from the soul of Christ went in upon them deeper and deeper. But there came a point when they went to pieces, when it could walk into their hearts no more, when to all appearance it would have faded into a spiritualized

Judaism, and that again into its common day, but for something which happened quite different from a rise to a new stage, something whose crisis was at Pentecost. No impression from the soul, or even from the teaching, of Christ, no memory of his wonderful works saved the disciples from desertion and betrayal. Disciples must become confessors, and confessors apostles. The disciples had had acting on them Christ's own confidence in his future, often and variously expressed, but they could not trust even that unique action of his soul on theirs. Under the crucifixion they broke down. They did not simply fail to rise: they forsook him and fled. It was only when the cross had its decisive, creative action as interpreted by the resurrection and by Penetecost that they came to themselves and to him for ever. Then they had something more to preach about than the way they were arrested and changed by the inner life of Jesus. Peter within a few weeks of his denial was converting crowds, and setting the lame man at the temple gate to leap and sing. What was the secret of the change, the miracle? It was not the mystery of Christ's abysmal personality, nor the magic atmosphere radiating from him, but the risen Christ and the Holy Ghost. It was by the power of the new life of Christ through the cross that Peter healed the cripple. The power that made this man walk was the same power that raised Christ from death; and raised him from no individual decease, but from the death which lay upon the whole world, for which he was made sin. Peter never really found his soul till he was incorporated into that death and resurrection of Christ. And he gives his own account of it thus: "God hath regenerated us into a living hope by the resurrection of Christ from the dead" (1 Peter 1:3). This is the mysticism of the cross, which is a different thing from the mysticism of the soul. Christianity is not the religion of personality merely, but of redemption.